C I T Y P A C K
Chicago

By Mick Sinclair

Fodor's
3RD EDITION

Fodor's Travel Publications
New York • Toronto • London • Sydney • Auckland

WWW.FODORS.COM

Contents

About this book 4

About this book

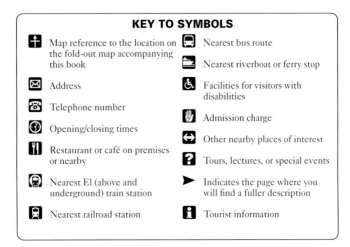

KEY TO SYMBOLS

+ Map reference to the location on the fold-out map accompanying this book

✉ Address

☎ Telephone number

🕐 Opening/closing times

🍴 Restaurant or café on premises or nearby

Ⓔ Nearest El (above and underground) train station

🚊 Nearest railroad station

🚌 Nearest bus route

⛴ Nearest riverboat or ferry stop

♿ Facilities for visitors with disabilities

✋ Admission charge

↔ Other nearby places of interest

? Tours, lectures, or special events

➤ Indicates the page where you will find a fuller description

ℹ Tourist information

Citypack Chicago is divided into six sections to cover the six most important aspects of your visit to Chicago. It includes:

- The city and its people
- Itineraries, walks, and excursions
- The top 25 sights to visit
- What makes the city special
- Restaurants, hotels, stores, and nightlife
- Practical information

In addition, easy-to-read side panels provide extra facts and snippets, highlights of places to visit, and invaluable practical advice.

CROSS-REFERENCES

To help you make the most of your visit, cross-references, indicated by ➤, show you where to find additional information about a place or subject.

MAPS

The fold-out map in the wallet at the back of the book is a comprehensive street plan of Chicago. All the map references given in the book refer to this map. For example, the Chicago Board of Trade on W. Jackson Boulevard has the following information: **+ 67**—indicating the grid square of the map in which the Chicago Board of Trade will be found.

The downtown maps found on the inside front and back covers of the book itself are for quick reference. They show the top 25 sights, described on pages 24–48, which are clearly plotted by number (**1** – **25**, not page number) from west to east.

ADMISSION CHARGES

An indication of the admission charge (for all attractions) is given by categorizing the standard adult rate as follows:

✋ expensive (over $13), moderate ($7–13), inexpensive (under $7).

CHICAGO
life

Introducing Chicago

Looking up at the El

Renamed El lines

During the mid-1990s, the various lines of Chicago's El (elevated railroad) were renamed according to colors. However, you are still likely to hear the old names, which usually refer to the end points of each route:

Green—Lake/Englewood/
Jackson Park

Brown—Ravenswood/Loop

Red—Howard/Dan Ryan

Purple—Linden /Howard
(rush hours only)

Blue—O'Hare/Congress/
Douglas

Orange—Midway Airport

Chicago has been called "the city that works." The fact is Chicago *has* to work. It is one of the dynamos driving the nation. Being the hub of transportation and trade between the East and West coasts spurred its growth through the 19th century. The city remains the major marketplace for the Midwest's multimillion dollar agricultural output and a venue for scores of major trade shows and conventions. Chicago's O'Hare is one of the world's busiest airports, so when rain, snow, fog, or other weather conditions affect the area air travel across much of the U.S. is paralyzed.

When it's not working hard, Chicago plays hard. The city has spawned football legends, such as the Chicago Bears' Mike Ditka, and basketball superstars such as the Chicago Bulls' Michael Jordan, whose retirement not long ago changed the face of American pro basketball. North Side baseball fans cheer the National League's Chicago Cubs playing on real grass at historic Wrigley Field, while their counterparts watch the American League's White Sox on the astroturf of Comiskey Park.

From Frank Lloyd Wright to Mies van der Rohe, every major modern architect has left a calling card in the "Windy City." The architectural pedigree stems from the fire of 1871, after which Chicago had to be built afresh. New steel-frame construction techniques, the invention of the elevator, and the booming city's need to make as much use as possible of a single plot of land, conspired to make Chicago the first city of skyscrapers. With their 20-story office blocks and department stores, design pioneers such as Daniel Burnham and Louis Sullivan—leading what became known worldwide as the Chicago School of Architecture—gave Chicago a unique skyline. A surprising number of early structures remain, among them the Carson Pirie Scott &

Co. store, the Rookery, and the Reliance Building, their terra-cotta facades overshadowed by the soaring glass and steel edifices that now sprout in the Loop, Chicago's business district. The technological ingenuity that enabled steadily higher construction climaxed in 1974 with the 110-story Sears Tower.

Like the archetypal American city, Chicago's growth has been the result of waves of immigration. Irish, Italians, Poles, and Germans were among the early arrivals from Europe whose labor contributed to the expansion of the city and whose presence is still apparent. St. Patrick's Day is one of the city's major annual festivals, and Chicago is one of the few U.S. cities where you may hear Ukrainian spoken on the street. Among the African-Americans who came from the Deep South were the musicians that created the distinctive musical style known as the Chicago blues and those that helped make the city a place of pilgrimage for the world's jazz fans.

Today's immigrants continue to shape the face of Chicago, with growing Hispanic enclaves—long-established Mexican-Americans were joined by arrivals from Central America—and more recently India, Korea, Thailand, and other parts of Southeast Asia.

Michael Jordan

Almost single-handedly responsible for the success of the Chicago Bulls, Michael Jordan is among basketball's all-time greats. Born in Brooklyn, Jordan joined the Bulls in 1984 and went on to top the NBA scoring charts for seven consecutive seasons. After leading the Bulls to six World Championships, he retired in 1999.

Oprah Winfrey

Born in Mississippi, Oprah Winfrey moved to Chicago in 1984 and turned a moribund morning chat show into the hugely successful Oprah Winfrey Show. Winfrey's groundbreaking discussions of emotional and social issues underpinned the show's popularity and made her a household name.

The Downtown skyline, seen across Grant Park

Studs Terkel

Born in New York in 1912, Studs Terkel arrived in Chicago as a child and later established himself as one of the city's most listened-to radio interviewers. Terkel's trademark style of allowing the interviewee to tell his or her own story largely unhindered continued into a string of internationally acclaimed books of oral history, among them *Division Street: America*, describing Chicago through the words of 70 of its citizens.

All settlers, past or present, find that Chicago makes demands. Climate alone necessitates an all-weather wardrobe almost all year round. Another necessity is an understanding of the strange ability of the Chicago Cubs and the White Sox to be unsuccessful season after season (the Cubs last won the World Series in 1908, the White Sox in 1917).

Chicago offers a horde of first-rate museums (among them the Chicago Historical Society and the Art Institute of Chicago), cultural activity the equal of the country's best, and shopping that not only rivals New York's but is often focused on architecturally inventive retail centers. Beaches belie the fact that Chicago is almost a thousand miles from the nearest ocean, and a nine-month-long program of major events takes place for free in the city's parks.

Chicagoans themselves appear refreshingly straightforward and friendly. A broad rivalry exists between North and South Siders, but more revealing is the fact that Chicago splits into 77 neighborhoods, each with its own looks and atmosphere. The abiding impression is that Chicagoans do not live in a city at all but in close-knit communities in a dense conglomeration of small towns—part of a metropolitan area that locals, without a trace of whimsy, refer to as "Chicagoland."

Above: A tiled street mural livens up the Loop, Chicago's financial district at the heart of the city

CHICAGO IN FIGURES

General Information
- Miles from New York: 724.
- Miles from San Francisco: 1,756.
- Miles from London: 4,167.
- Miles from Berlin: 4,793.
- Population: 2.86 million; third-largest city in the United States.
- Area: 228½ sq miles.
- Miles of street: 3,776.
- Miles of lake front: 29.
- Miles of beaches: 31.
- Miles of lakefront bicycle paths: 18.
- Parks: 551.

Geography
- Latitude: N 41° 50'.
- Longitude: W 87° 45'.
- Highest point: 672 feet above sea level.

Lake Michigan
- Length: 321 miles.
- Width: 118 miles.
- Shoreline: 1,638 miles.
- Average depth: 279 feet.
- Greatest depth: 923 feet.

Architecture
- Tallest buildings: Sears Tower (1,454 feet), Amoco Building (1,136 feet), John Hancock Center (1,127 feet).
- Building with largest floor space: the Merchandise Mart, 90 acres.
- Movable bridges: 50l.

Weather
- Hottest day recorded: 105°F, July 24, 1934.
- Coldest day recorded: -27°F, January 20, 1985.
- Fastest wind gust recorded: 69mph, April 29, 1984.
- Windiest months: March and April.
- Wettest month: June.
- Hottest month: July.

Trivia
- Chicago's Lyon & Healy is the world's oldest maker of standing string harps.
- Chicago's Nabisco has the world's largest cookie and cracker factory.
- Chicago's firm of William Wrigley, Jr., is the world's biggest chewing gum manufacturer.

A Chronology

1673	Jacques Marquette and Louis Joliet discover the 1½-mile Native American portage trail linking the Mississippi River and the Great Lakes—the site of future Chicago.
1779–1781	Trapper and trader Jean-Baptiste Point Du Sable, a Haitian of African and French descent, becomes the first non-native settler.
1812	Fort Dearborn, one of several forts protecting trade routes, is attacked by Native Americans. Some 50 of its occupants die.
1830	Chicago is selected as the site of a canal linking the Great Lakes and the Mississippi.
1850	Chicago's population reaches 30,000 (300 in 1830). Many arrivals are Irish, who find work building the Midwest's railroads.
1870	Chicago's population reaches 300,000.
1871	The Great Fire (► 12).
1886	The Haymarket Riot (► 12). At a workers' rally, police open fire on the crowd. The trial and executions that follow are condemned by labor movements worldwide.
1893	Chicago hosts the World's Columbian Exposition. The hyperbole of business leaders causes a visiting journalist to describe Chicago as "the windy city," an enduring epithet.
1894	A strike at the Pullman rail company unites black and white workers for the first time.
1906	Upton Sinclair's novel *The Jungle* focuses national attention on the conditions endured by workers in the Union Stockyards, a notorious slaughterhouse and packing complex.
1908	Chicago Cubs win baseball's World Series for a second successive year, following the success of the Chicago White Sox in 1906.

1914 | With World War I, Chicago's black population increases further as African-Americans from the Deep South move north to industrial jobs.

1919–1933 | Prohibition. Excellent transportation links make Chicago a natural center for liquor manufacture and distribution. Armed crime mobs thrive.

1950s | In South Side clubs, rhythmic and electrified Chicago blues evolves. Muddy Waters and John Lee Hooker are prime exponents.

1955 | Richard J. Daley is elected mayor, and dominates Chicago political life for 21 years.

1968 | Police attack Anti-Vietnam War protesters in Grant Park during the Democratic National Convention, an event seen on TV by millions.

1974 | Completion of Sears Tower, the world's tallest building until 1996.

Late 1980s | DJs at Chicago's Warehouse nightclub create "house music," inspiring a worldwide dance-music explosion.

1989 | Richard M. Daley, son of Richard J., is elected mayor.

1992 | A collapsing wall causes the Chicago River to flood the Loop, paralyzing the business district for two weeks.

1995 | A heatwave kills 700 people.

1997 | Cabbies strike over the law requiring them to pick up all fares and serve all areas of the city.

1998 | Chicago Cubs' Sammy Sosa beats the 37-year record for the most home runs in a season, a week after the St. Louis Cardinals' Mark McGuire achieves the same feat.

1999 | After helping the Bulls to their sixth NBA championship since 1991, Michael Jordan retires.

11

PEOPLE & EVENTS FROM HISTORY

Richard J. Daley

With 60,000 jobs in what he dubbed the "Machine" of the city administration either directly appointed or greatly influenced by him, Richard J. Daley (aka "The Boss") dominated Chicago politics from 1955 until 1976. Daley won the favor of big business but was loathed elsewhere for his autocratic style and readiness to use force, most notoriously against demonstrators at the 1968 Democratic Convention.

Chicago's legendary mobster, Al Capone

THE GREAT FIRE

The summer of 1871 had been exceptionally hot and dry, with many forest fires in the Chicago area. On October 8, warm winds caused a fire in the southwest of the city to spread rapidly. Crashing meteors, a dropped match, and Mrs O'Leary's cow (said to have kicked over a lantern in its barn) are among the many theories and legends on how the fire started. The fire jumped the Chicago River, and blazed for two days through a city whose firefighting capacity had failed to keep pace with the city's growth. Before it was extinguished by judiciously used gunpowder and the heavy rain, the fire claimed 250 lives, razed nearly 18,000 buildings over 4sq miles, and rendered over 90,000 people homeless.

THE HAYMARKET RIOT

Heavy-handed police tactics in a series of labor disputes prompted a group of German-born anarchists to organize a protest rally on May 4, 1886, in Haymarket Square. A bomb thrown from the crowd exploded among the police lines; the explosion and the police use of firearms killed seven people and wounded 150. As a result, seven anarchists received death sentences. In 1893, a full pardon was granted to three anarchists serving prison terms, due to the lack of evidence linking any anarchists to the bomb.

GANGSTERS

Intended to encourage sobriety and family life, Prohibition (1919–1933) provided a great stimulus to organized crime. The exploits of Chicago-based gangsters such as Al Capone became legendary. Though depicted frequently in movies and on TV, shoot-outs between rival gangs were rare. An exception was the 1929 St. Valentine Day's Massacre, when Capone's gang eliminated their archrivals in a hail of machine-gun fire. Wealthy enough to bribe corruptible politicians and police, the gangsters seemed invincible, but the gangster-era—though not necessarily the gangs—ended with the imprisonment of Capone in 1931, and the repeal of Prohibition.

CHICAGO
how to organize your time

ITINERARIES

Chicago is best seen on foot. Walking between neighborhoods in and around the Loop is safe and easy, although forays further afield require a car or travel on the city's comprehensive network of buses, El trains, and, less often, Metra commuter trains.

ITINERARY ONE	**THE LOOP AND ART INSTITUTE OF CHICAGO**
Morning	Wait for the rush hour to subside and begin a walk around the Loop. Take in the many points of historic and architectural interest: start at Sears Tower and head steadily eastward.
Lunch	Berghoff Restaurant (► 68) or Russian Tea Time (► 68).
Afternoon	Complete your tour of the Loop and cross into Grant Park (► 41). Spend the rest of the day at the Art Institute of Chicago (► 40) or simply strolling in the park. Alternatively, take public transportation to the Jane Addams Hull-House Museum (► 26).
ITINERARY TWO	**THE MAGNIFICENT MILE AND VICINITY**
Morning	From the Michigan Avenue Bridge, view the Wrigley Building and Tribune Tower, and then go north past the glitzy stores of the Magnificent Mile (► 51). Tour the Terra Museum of American Art (► 36), then continue to the elegant houses along the Gold Coast (► 50, panel).
Lunch	Gino's East (► 65) or Tempo (► 69).
Afternoon	Continue northward by bus to Lincoln Park (► 29). Spend the rest of the day there, visiting the zoo (► 29 and 59), conservatory, beaches, and other attractions, according to your taste and the weather. In the south of the park is the Chicago Historical Society (► 33). Alternatively, return south and spend the afternoon visiting Navy Pier (► 60), where dense crowds can be expected on weekends.

ITINERARY THREE	**MAJOR MUSEUMS AND GRACELAND CEMETERY OR WRIGLEY FIELD**
Morning	Spend the whole day visiting the Field Museum of Natural History (➤ 42), the John G. Shedd Aquarium (➤ 44), and the Adler Planetarium and its astronomical exhibits (➤ 46). All three are excellent for children. Or select one or two of these museums and spend the afternoon as detailed below.
Lunch	Soundings Restaurant (➤ 44), or a picnic in Grant Park (➤ 41).
Afternoon	Take public transportation south to the University of Chicago campus to visit the Oriental Institute (➤ 47), followed by the Du Sable Museum of African-American History (➤ 45). If you have children with you, the Museum of Science and Industry (➤ 48) is a better stop. Or take public transportation north to tour Graceland Cemetery (➤ 27); or go to watch the Chicago Cubs play at Wrigley Field (➤ 28, April to October—check game times).
ITINERARY FOUR	**UKRAINIAN AND POLISH CHICAGO, AND OAK PARK**
Morning	Take public transportation to the Ukrainian Village (➤ 51). Explore the Village, where you'll find St. Nicholas Cathedral (➤ 56), which serves the Ukrainian community, and the Ukrainian Culture Center. Continue to the Polish Museum of America (➤ 25).
Lunch	Sak's Ukrainian Village Restaurant (➤ 68) or, on a weekend, Mareva's (➤ 68).
Afternoon	Take public transportation to Oak Park. Visit the Frank Lloyd Wright Home & Studio (➤ 24) and Unity Temple (➤ 56), also designed by Frank Lloyd Wright. Stroll past the many other buildings of architectural and historic interest in the vicinity, including the birthplace of, and the museum devoted to, writer Ernest Hemingway (➤ 53).

15

WALKS

Dubuffet's Monument with Standing Beast

INFORMATION

Distance Approx 1½ miles
Time 2–3 hours
Start point Sears Tower
🚇 G7
🚆 Brown and Orange lines: Quincy
🚌 1, 60, 151, 156
End point Chicago Cultural Center
🚇 H6
🚆 Brown and Orange lines: Madison
🚌 3, 4, 60, 145, 147, 151

THE WEST LOOP

Begin at Sears Tower (1974), until 1996 the world's tallest building, with a fantastic view from its 103rd-floor Skydeck. Continue along Jackson Boulevard for the Chicago Board of Trade (1930), observing the trading from the visitors' gallery. Turn north along La Salle Street and peek inside the architecturally stunning Rookery (1880s). Continue north to the junction with Randolph Street to view the James R. Thompson Center (formerly known as the State of Illinois Center, and built in 1985), which has the Dubuffet sculpture, *Monument with Standing Beast*, looming outside. Inside, the 17-story atrium echoes the building's curvilinear exterior and allows natural light to flood the interior. Cross Randolph Street to look inside the Richard J. Daley Center (1965). Leave by the Washington Street side to view the 50-foot-tall untitled Picasso sculpture made from 162 tons of steel, opposite which is Joan Miro's sculpture of "Chicago."

Lunch and snacks Food stands lining the lower level of the James R. Thompson Center offer various fast food. The Berghoff Restaurant (➤ 68), a Chicago institution, serves hearty German fare. On the first floor of the Chicago Cultural Center is a café serving good coffee and snacks.

THE EAST LOOP

Stroll south along the increasingly tree-lined State Street, passing the glass and terra-cotta Reliance Building (1890s). Check out Miró's sculpture, *Chicago*, marking the plaza of 69 W. Washington Street. Continue to Louis Sullivan's exquisite, early 20th-century Carson Pirie Scott & Co. building, and cross to Dearborn Street for the Marquette Building (1895). Resume walking south to the Harold Washington Library Center. End the walk by strolling north along Michigan Avenue to the Chicago Cultural Center (1897), at the junction with Washington Street.

THE MAGNIFICENT MILE: SOUTH

Leave the Loop by walking north across the Chicago River on Michigan Avenue Bridge, which in 1920 facilitated the rise of the so-called Magnificent Mile as a fashionable retail and commercial area. Two of the first structures erected after the bridge was built were the Wrigley Building (1921/1924), to the left, and the Tribune Tower (1925), to the right. Farther north, opulent stores and hotels line Michigan Avenue. One of the liveliest stores is Nike Town, a retail showplace of the sports clothing manufacturer, between Erie and Huron streets. Cross to the west side of Michigan Avenue to see the excellent Terra Museum of American Art.

Lunch The Billy Goat Tavern (➤ 83) offers burgers and similar snacks. Pizzeria Uno (➤ 65, panel) is *the* place for deep-dish pizza. For more exotic fare, try Szechwan East (➤ 67), or the weekday lunch buffet at Bukhara (➤ 66).

THE MAGNIFICENT MILE: NORTH

Continue to the junction with Chicago Avenue and stop at the Historic Water Tower. Built in 1869 to house water-pumping equipment, the tower survived the fire and now holds a photographic gallery. A block north, on the junction with Chestnut Street, is the imposing Gothic form of the Fourth Presbyterian Church, used for lunchtime recitals. A short distance west, on Chestnut Street, there is more Gothic exuberance at the Quigley Seminary (1920s). Return to and cross Michigan Avenue to Water Tower Place, a glitzy, high-profile shopping mall. Across Delaware Place is the Palmolive Building, a 1930 art-deco landmark. Finish the walk at the John Hancock Center (1970), whose 94th-floor observatory affords stunning views across Chicago.

THE SIGHTS

- Wrigley Building (➤ 35)
- Tribune Tower (➤ 39)
- Terra Museum of American Art (➤ 36)
- Historic Water Tower (➤ 54)
- Fourth Presbyterian Church (➤ 56)
- Quigley Seminary (➤ 56)
- John Hancock Center (➤ 55)

INFORMATION

Distance 1 mile
Time 2–3 hours
Start point Michigan Avenue Bridge
🚇 H5/6
🚊 Red line: Grand
🚌 3, 11, 29, 65, 147, 151, 157
End point John Hancock Center
🚇 H4
🚊 Red line: Chicago
🚌 145, 146, 147, 151

View from the John Hancock Center

Evenings Out

*City nightlife: the lights
of Downtown Chicago*

An evening out on the town in Chicago can span bar-hopping and nightclubbing, listening to live music, or simply strolling by late-opening stores. Several neighborhoods are particularly interesting at night.

RIVER NORTH AND RIVER WEST

In this area immediately north of the Loop, numerous restaurants do double duty as nightlife venues. Here are branches of the theme restaurant chains Hard Rock Café and Rainforest Café, and their lesser-known local rivals. Across the Chicago River, where a few old warehouses mark River West, are more top-rated nightspots, though the area is not suitable for casual evening strolling.

RUSH AND DIVISION STREETS

Although River North and River West have taken away some of the area's customers, the northern section of Rush Street (close to Division Street), near the Loop and many hotels, is long-established as a nightlife area with bars, restaurants, small music venues, and dance clubs. The abundance of nightspots and the area's compact size make it a good place to club-hop.

WRIGLEYVILLE/LAKE VIEW

These two neighborhoods (several miles north of the Loop, but easy to reach by El train or bus), which have increasingly been settled by liberal-minded Chicagoans in their mid-20s and 30s, hold most of the newer and more alternative-minded live-music spots and clubs, as well as all manner of bars and cafés. The city's main concentration of gay and lesbian nightspots is also here. Most activity is along Belmont Avenue, Broadway, and Clark Street, and to a lesser extent along Sheffield, Halsted, and Lincoln avenues.

INFORMATION

River North and River West
- ✚ F/G4/5
- 🚇 Brown line: Chicago. Red line: Grand, Chicago
- 🚌 22, 37, 41, 65, 66

Rush and Division streets
- ✚ G/H4
- 🚇 Red line: Clark/Division
- 🚌 36, 70

Wrigleyville/Lake View
- ✚ Off map to north
- 🚇 Brown and Red lines: Belmont. Red line: Addison
- 🚌 22, 36, 77, 151, 152

ORGANIZED SIGHTSEEING

WALKING TOURS

Chicago Architecture Foundation ☎ 312/922–TOUR
Two-hour walking tours of the Loop's landmark
buildings and, some Sunday mornings, guided
walks through Graceland Cemetery.

BOAT TOURS

Chicago Architecture Foundation ☎ 312/922–TOUR
A 90-minute narrated boat trip to view the archi-
tecturally significant buildings lining the
Chicago River.

Chicago's First Lady ☎ 847/358–1330 Narrated
voyage past some of the Loop's best architecture, including lunch or dinner; a "lunch magic"
cruise features a magician.

Mercury, Chicago's Skyline Cruiseline ☎ 312/332–1353
A choice of one- to two-hour cruises, some
specializing in history or architecture. Includes
the Chicago River and Lake Michigan.

Spirit of Chicago ☎ 312/836–7899 Lunch or dinner,
or dinner-and-dance trips
on Lake Michigan.

BUS TOURS

Chicago Trolley Company
☎ 312/663–0260 and the
**Chicago Motor Coach
Company** ☎ 312/663–1000
Both operate guided tours
in and around the Loop;
ticket-holders can hop on
and off at marked stops.

**Chicago Architecture
Foundation** ☎ 312/922–3432
A choice of bus tours concentrating on general
architectural highlights, the buildings of Frank
Lloyd Wright, or historic homes.

Tour Black Chicago ☎ 312/332–TOUR This tour
reveals a century of African-American culture in
Chicago, concentrating on South Side neighborhoods such as Bronzeville and the Pullman
District.

The Party Bus ☎ 312/266–7330 On Fridays and
Saturdays, this double-decker bus ferries its
passengers to four Chicago nightclubs; no cover
charges or lines to enter clubs.

Air tours and carriage rides

One of the few ways to get
higher than Chicago's towering
buildings is by taking a small
plane or helicopter tour. Chicago
By Air (☎ 708/524–1172)
offers a half-hour swoop above
the city in a single-engined
plane. By contrast, The Noble
Horse (☎ 312/266–7878)
provides the chance to ride a
horsedrawn buggy along the
Magnificent Mile.

*Traveling in style along
Michigan Avenue*

EXCURSIONS

North Shore
Distance From the Loop: Evanston
12 miles; Wilmette 16 miles;
Chicago Botanic Gardens
25 miles
Journey time Evanston 20–30
minutes; Wilmette 25–35
minutes; Chicago Botanic
Gardens 35–40 minutes
🚇 Evanston or Davis

Block Museum of Art
✉ Northwestern University,
1967 S. Campus Drive,
Evanston
☎ 847/491–4000
🕐 Tue–Wed noon–5; Thu–Sun
noon–8
✋ Free

Grosse Point Lighthouse
✉ 2601 Sheridan Road,
Evanston
☎ 847/328–6961
🕐 Jun–Sep: daily 2–5
✋ Moderate

Baha'i House of Worship
✉ 100 Linden Avenue,
Wilmette
☎ 847/853–2300
🕐 May–Sep: daily 10–10.
Oct–Apr: daily 10–5
🚇 Wilmette
✋ Free

Chicago Botanic Gardens
✉ 1000 Lake-Cook Road,
Glencoe (take I-94 north)
☎ 847/835–5440
🕐 Daily 8AM–sunset
✋ Moderate

NORTH SHORE

The communities lining Lake Michigan north of Chicago are best toured as a whole by car, though numerous individual places of interest are easily reached by public transportation.

Evanston, Chicago's oldest and largest suburb, has upscale stores that lure many city-dwellers on weekend buying expeditions, and its two historic districts of 19th-century residences are pleasant. Evanston is also the site of Northwestern University, whose Block Museum of Art mounts excellent art exhibitions. The lake front immediately north of the university is ideal for strolling and picnicking. Make for the 1873 Grosse Point Lighthouse and enjoy the splendid lake view from its 113-foot-high tower.

Continuing north, Wilmette holds the Mosque-like, dome-topped Baha'i House of Worship, built over 40 years from 1920 and the first temple in the United States for this religion, originally from Iran. Farther north near Glencoe, in the 385-acre Chicago Botanic Gardens, landscaped pathways link carefully nurtured English Rose, Japanese Island, and Prairie gardens.

PULLMAN

Built in the 1880s for the 11,000 workers of the Pullman company (known for its railroad cars), Pullman was protected as a National Historic Landmark in 1971, and many of its 1,800 original buildings remain. Take the Metra train to Pullman; by car, take Dan Ryan and Calumet expressways south, exiting west at 111th Street.

The creation of the town, although apparently an act of paternalism by company owner George M. Pullman, was inspired in part by a wish to keep his workforce away from the influence of Chicago's organized labor movement. Ironically, the company's failure to lower rents in line with wage cuts, among other grievances, led to the celebrated Pullman strike of 1894.

WESTERN SUBURBS

If you have a car, a couple of other attractions are worth your while. Closest is Brookfield Zoo, 14 miles from the city in the town of Brookfield. With 2,500 creatures spread across 215 acres of replicated habitat, including an indoor rain forest, the zoo is enjoyable for a few hours, particularly for children. Without youngsters to please, a better stop is the Morton Arboretum, in Lisle, 25 miles from the city. Landscaped woodlands, wetlands, and prairie are spread across 1,500 acres crisscrossed by foot trails and a 12-mile road tour route. Farther west, via I-88 and State Route 31, the idyllic small towns of St. Charles, Geneva, and Batavia line the Fox River, each with a generous endowment of antiques stores and preserved historic buildings.

SIX FLAGS GREAT AMERICA

Gurnee, west of the city, is the home of Six Flags Great America, the Midwest's largest theme park, where in its five historically themed areas you will find exciting high-rise rollercoasters that reach speeds of 65mph, and other thrill rides—including a few for small children—plus spectacular shows, parades, and special events. Be sure to sample the 996-seat Pictorium Theater, a breathtaking experience where films of action stunts, natural phenomena, and much more are projected with frightening realism onto a gigantic (70 foot by 96 foot) IMAX screen.

INFORMATION

Historic Pullman Foundation Visitors Center
- ✉ 11141 S. Cottage Grove Avenue
- ☎ 773/785–8181

Brookfield Zoo
Distance 14 miles from the Loop
Journey time 20–30 minutes
- ✉ 1st Avenue and 31st Street, Brookfield
- ☎ 708/485–2200
- 🕐 Sep–May: daily 10–4:30. Jun–Aug: daily 9:30–5:30
- 💲 Moderate; free Oct–Mar Tue and Thu

Morton Arboretum
Distance 25 miles from the Loop
Journey time 50–60 minutes
- ✉ On State Route 50, Lisle
- ☎ 603/968–0074
- 🕐 Daily 7–7
- 💲 Moderate

Six Flags Great America
Distance 43 miles from the Loop
Journey time 70–90 minutes
- ✉ Gurnee, accessed from I-94 at 132 E. Grand Avenue exit
- ☎ 847/249–1776
- 🕐 Late Apr–Aug: daily 10–5/6/7/8/9/10. Early Sep: Sat–Sun 10–8/9
- 💲 Expensive (rides included in admission price)

WHAT'S ON

Whether it is a major museum exhibition or a neighborhood get-together, something special is happening in Chicago almost every week of the year. A free quarterly booklet, *Chicago Calendar of Events*, can be picked up at one of the city's three visitor centers (► 90). Other sources for what's-on information are the Friday *Chicago Tribune*, *Chicago* magazine, and the weekly free newspapers, *Reader* and *New City*.

January/February	*Chinese New Year*: Celebrated in Chinatown.
March	*St. Patrick's Day*: The whole city, including the Chicago River, turns green, and there's a parade through the Loop.
April	*Spring flower shows*: Lincoln Park and Garfield Park conservatories.
May	*Polish Constitution Day* (May 7): Chicago's many Polish-Americans celebrate with a parade in the Loop and other events focusing on Polish culture.
	Wright Plus: Once-a-year chance to see inside private Oak Park homes designed by Frank Lloyd Wright.
June	*Chicago Blues Festival*: Local and international artists perform for massive audiences in Grant Park.
	Printer's Row Book Fair: Used-book stores offer bargains and host special events.
	Chicago Gospel Festival: Gospel music in Grant Park.
July	*Taste of Chicago*: A feeding frenzy; in the 11 days leading up to July 4, thousands sample dishes from city restaurants. It ends with a firework display.
	Independence Day (July 4): Special events such as firework displays, the largest taking place in Grant Park.
August	*Ravinia Festival* (from mid-June through Labor Day): Two months of the Chicago Symphony Orchestra, plays, and other cultural events, with picnicking on the lawns.
	Chicago Air & Water Show: Spectacular stunts performed off North Avenue Beach.
September	*Chicago Jazz Festival*: International jazz stars headline free concerts in Grant Park.
October	*Chicago Marathon*: 26-mile run through the city, beginning and ending in Grant Park.
November	*Festival of Lights:* 30,000 lights illuminate the Magnificent Mile for the Christmas season.

CHICAGO's
top 25 sights

The sights are shown on the maps on the inside front cover and inside back cover, numbered **1–25** *from west to east across the city*

FRANK LLOYD WRIGHT HOME & STUDIO

DID YOU KNOW?

- 1867 Frank Lloyd Wright born in Wisconsin
- 1887 Arrives in Chicago
- 1909 Leaves Chicago to spend a year in Europe
- 1910 Opens Taliesin, a home and architectural school in Wisconsin
- 1936 Designs Fallingwater—a family home extending over a waterfall in a forest near Pittsburgh; a masterpiece of organic architecture
- 1938 Taliesin West, a winter home and school, opens in Arizona
- 1943 Finishes plans for New York's Guggenheim Museum; completed 16 years later
- 1959 Dies

INFORMATION

- ✚ Off map to west
- ✉ 951 Chicago Avenue, Oak Park
- ☎ 708/848–1976
- ◷ Guided tours only: Mon–Fri 11, 1, 3; Sat–Sun 11–3:30 continuously
- Ⓠ Green line: Harlem
- 🚏 Oak Park
- 🚌 23
- ♿ Few
- 💲 Moderate
- ↔ Hemingway Museum (► 53), Unity Temple (► 56)

Frank Lloyd Wright's Drafting Room

An insight into the early ideas of one of the greatest and most influential architects of the 20th century. It is an essential stop for anyone interested in design, or in the ability of one man to realize his extraordinary vision.

Organic ideas Working for the Chicago architect Louis Sullivan, the 22-year-old Frank Lloyd Wright designed this home in 1889 for himself, his first wife, and their children, and furnished it with his own pieces. The shingled exterior is not typical of Wright but the bold geometric shape stands out among the neighboring Queen Anne-style houses. Inside, the open plan, central fireplaces, and low ceilings are the earliest examples of the elements that became fundamental in Wright's so-called Prairie School of Architecture. Particularly notable are the children's playroom, the high-backed chairs in the dining room, and the willow tree that grows through the walls in keeping with Wright's theory of organic architecture—architecture in harmony with its natural surroundings.

Prairie views In 1893, Wright opened his own practice in an annex to the house: a concealed entrance leads into an office showcasing many of Wright's ideas, such as suspended lamps and an open-plan work space. The draftsmen once employed here on seminal Prairie School buildings worked in a stunningly designed room in sight of what was then open prairie.

POLISH MUSEUM OF AMERICA

While this museum does not document Chicago's Polish community specifically, it does enable many Chicago Poles to trace their roots. It is also home to Polish cultural treasures threatened during the troubled post-World War II years.

History East Europeans have long had a strong presence in Chicago, but no group among them has had greater visibility than Polish-Americans. Stanislow Batowski's immense painting, *Pulaski at Savannah*, dominates the museum's main room and sets off the collections remembering Pulaski and Koscziusko, two Polish soldiers who played significant roles in the American Revolution. The former was killed in battle and the latter helped lead the 1794 Polish uprising against Russia. Nearby are folk costumes, decorated Easter eggs, the costumes of the celebrated Shakespearean actress Helena Modrzejewska, and remnants of the first Polish church in the United States.

Artistry Modestly occupying a corner is the immense stained-glass window that formed the centerpiece of the Polish culture exhibition at the 1939 New York World's Fair, its return home halted by the outbreak of war in Europe. The stairways and an upper floor are lined by Polish art, old and new. Amid many fine graphic works, look out for Mrozewski's cryptic 1936 depiction of H.G. Wells. A separate room holds mementoes of Ignaczi Jan Paderewski, the pianist and composer whose U. S. concert raised funds in the struggle for Polish independence in the early 1900s and who, in 1919, became the first prime minister of the Polish Republic. The last piano on which Paderewski performed is on display here, and so is the chair he used for all his performances.

DID YOU KNOW?

- 1851 Anton Smarzewski becomes Chicago's first Polish settler
- 1864 Peter Kiolbasa arrives in Chicago from Texas; entering public life, he becomes the city's first well-known Polish-American; he is nicknamed "honest Pete"
- 1869 Chicago's first Roman Catholic parish is established by Polish settlers
- 1871 German oppression of Poles causes a great rise in emigration to the U.S. Many settle in Chicago
- 1920 Poles become Chicago's largest foreign-born ethnic group
- 1937 Polish Museum opens

INFORMATION

- ✚ E4
- ✉ 984 N. Milwaukee Avenue
- ☎ 773/384–3352
- 🕐 Daily 11–4
- Blue line: Division
- 🚌 9, 41, 56
- ♿ Few
- 🎫 Donation
- ↔ Ukrainian Village (▶ 51)

JANE ADDAMS HULL-HOUSE MUSEUM

DID YOU KNOW?

- 1860 Jane Addams born in Cedarville, Illinois
- 1888 Visits England
- 1889 Opens Hull House with college friend Ellen Gates Starr
- 1909 Helps founding of National Association for Advancement of Colored People (NAACP)
- 1920 Helps founding of American Civil Liberties Union
- 1931 First American woman to receive Nobel Peace Prize
- 1935 Dies

INFORMATION

- F7
- 800 S. Halsted Street
- 312/413–5353
- Mon–Fri 10–4; Sun noon–5
- Blue line: UIC-Halsted
- Halsted
- 8
- Fair
- Free

An impoverished immigrant's grim lot was made less miserable by the work of Jane Addams. In the late 19th century she created Hull House, a community and center in one of the city's neediest neighborhoods—and sparked many of the U.S.'s earliest social reforms.

A better life Inspired by a visit to London's East End, Jane Addams founded Hull House in 1889, offering English-language and U.S. citizenship courses, child care, music and art classes, and other services to the area's disparate ethnic groups—Germans, Irish, Poles, Ukrainians, Lithuanians, and many more. She also campaigned, with much success, for improved sanitation, the end of child labor, a minimum wage, improved working conditions in factories, and for numerous other causes. Serving some 9,000 people each week at its peak, Hull House grew into a complex of 13 buildings. The two buildings that remain sit elegantly, if incongruously, on the geometrically complex campus of the University of Illinois, most of which was designed by Walter Mesch of Skidmore, Owings, & Merrill.

Prizewinning A 15-minute slide show tells the story of Addams and her settlement house, while the rooms of the main building are lined by furnishings and memorabilia including letters, photos, awards, and books from the house library (which began with Addams's old college books). These items chart the course of Hull House's growth, its vital role in Chicago, and the work that helped make Addams the most famous woman in America by the time she received the Nobel Peace Prize in 1931. The upper floor houses temporary exhibitions.

GRACELAND CEMETERY

Founded in 1860, Graceland is Chicago's most prestigious cemetery, the last resting place of many of the city's most influential citizens. Alongside great Chicagoans are a host of others, both famous and infamous.

Tombstone architecture Overlooked by high-rise lakeview apartments, its silence periodically broken by clattering El trains, this is a distinguished place to be buried. Even here, noted city architect Louis Sullivan has left a mark with his elegant and ornate 1890 tomb for the steel magnate Henry Getty and his family. Sullivan is himself a Graceland resident, as are other Chicago architects including Daniel Burnham, his partner, John Root, and modernist Ludwig Mies van der Rohe. Railroad-car manufacturer George Pullman is monumentalized by one of the largest tombs. Pullman died just three years after his workforce's bitter strike in 1894 (▶ 21), and his grave was covered by tons of concrete to deter desecration.

Odd graves Among countless oddities to seek out (the free map issued from the office is an essential tool) are the baseball adorning the resting place of National League co-founder William A. Hulbert and the unnerving statue, *Eternal Silence* by Laredo Taft, marking the tomb of hotel owner Dexter Graves.

DID YOU KNOW?

Also at Graceland:
- Philip D. Armour (meat-packing mogul)
- Marshall Field (department-store founder)
- Bob Fitzsimmons (boxer)
- Jack Johnson (boxer)
- John Kinzie (fur trapper, early settler)
- Victor Lawson (newspaper publisher)
- Cyrus H. McCormick (farm-machinery millionaire)
- Potter Palmer (property tycoon)
- Bertha Palmer (wife of Potter, and society queen)

INFORMATION

- ✚ Off map to north
- ✉ 4001 N. Clark Street
- ☎ 312/525–1105
- 🕐 Office: Mon–Sat 8:30–4. Gates open during daylight hours
- Ⓢ Brown line: Irving Park. Red line: Sheridan
- 🚌 80
- ♿ Good
- 🎟 Free
- ↔ Wrigley Field (▶ 28), Lincoln Park (▶ 29)
- ❓ Guided walking tours operated Aug–Sep by the Chicago Architecture Foundation (☎ 312/922–3432)

Daniel Burnham's grave

WRIGLEY FIELD

The days of successive World Series wins may be a distant memory, but the baseball of the Chicago Cubs and the defiantly unmodern form of their Wrigley Field stadium is as much a part of Chicago as the Water Tower and the elevated railroad.

Landmark With its ivy-covered brick outfield wall, Wrigley Field provides the perfect setting for America's traditional pastime. Built in 1914, the stadium has steadily resisted Astroturf, and the game takes place on grass within an otherwise perfectly ordinary city neighborhood, now known as Wrigleyville. Denied car-parking space, most spectators have to endure densely packed El trains to reach the ballpark. Seating on the eastern side of Wrigley Field is single-tier and unroofed, exposing dedicated Cubs fans to the vagaries of Chicago weather, which during the April to October season can encompass anything from snow to sunshine and 100°F temperatures.

Tradition Nearby residents watch the game from their windows, and some convert their roof space to box-like seating and charge admission. Others rent out their driveways as parking lots. Above the seats is the much-loved 1937 scoreboard on which the numbers are moved not by computer chips but by human hands. The floodlights did not appear until 1988, and then only after a fierce campaign of resistance. Someone in a high place may have objected: the first night game was abandoned because of rain.

DID YOU KNOW?

- Original name: Weeghman Park
- Original capacity: 14,000
- Original building cost: $250,000
- First occupants: Chicago Whales
- First National League game: April 1916
- Renamed: Cubs Park, 1920
- Renamed again: Wrigley Field, after owner William Wrigley, Jr., 1926
- Seating capacity: 38,765
- Nickname: "the friendly confines"

INFORMATION

- ✛ Off map to north
- ✉ 1060 W. Addison Street
- ☎ 773/404–2827
- Games: Apr–early Oct
- Fast-food stands; three restaurants
- Red line: Addison
- 22, 152
- Good
- Tickets moderate to expensive
- Graceland Cemetery (► 27)

LINCOLN PARK

This 6-mile-long, 1,200-acre green belt between the city and Lake Michigan has beaches, a zoo, a conservatory, a feast of statuary, and much more. The park attracts Chicagoans of all kinds in both winter and summer.

Small beginnings Created out of sand dunes, swamp, and the former city cemetery, Lincoln Park was established by the 1870s after its zoo (► 59) had been started with the gift of two swans from New York's Central Park. Evolving over a number of years through the contributions of various designers, it is now the oldest and most visited park in the United States. The gemlike 35-acre zoo houses lions, elephants, apes, polar bears, and penguins in replicated habitats; close by, the Conservatory (1891) encompasses four separate greenhouses. Invitingly warm on cool and breezy Chicago days, the greenhouses provide balmy temperatures for dazzling tropical and subtropical blooms and seasonal displays.

Beaches and bodies Tennis and badminton courts, putting greens, and ponds navigable in rented paddleboats are dotted across the rest of the park, linked by walking, jogging, and bike tracks. Facing the lake are several small beaches, crowded on sunny weekends. At the south end of the park are the Chicago Historical Society (► 33), and the Couch Mausoleum, which holds a few of the 20,000 corpses once buried beneath the park's southernmost reaches.

HIGHLIGHTS

- Lincoln Park Zoo
- The Conservatory
- Bates Fountain (conservatory garden)
- The Standing Lincoln
- Couch Mausoleum
- Beaches

Abraham Lincoln's statue in Lincoln Park

INFORMATION

- ✚ G/H1/2/3 and off map
- ✉ North of North Avenue, lining Lake Michigan
- ☎ Conservatory: 312/742–7737. Zoo: 312/742–2000
- ◉ Visit during daylight only
- 🍴 Cafeteria
- Ⓡ Red line: Armitage. Brown line: Fullerton (for zoo)
- 🚌 76, 77, 145, 146, 147, 151, 156
- ♿ Good
- 🎟 Free (including zoo)
- ↔ Chicago Historical Society (► 33)

29

SEARS TOWER

Although it is no longer the world's tallest building, the Sears Tower does rise higher than any other structure in this city. In addition to the unique and stylish architecture, it has the highest man-made vantage point in the western hemisphere.

Built from tubes From 1974 to 1996, the Sears Tower's 110 stories and 1,454-foot height made it the tallest building in the world, rising from the Loop with a distinctive profile of black aluminum and bronze-tinted glass. Working for the firm of Skidmore, Owings, & Merrill, architect Bruce Graham structured it around nine 75sq-foot bundled tubes, which decline in number as the building reaches upward. Aside from increasing the colossal structure's strength, this technique also echoes the stepback New York skyscraper style of the late 1920s. Among the early tasks during the three-year construction was the creation of foundation supports capable of holding a 222,500-ton building. At the opposite end, the two rooftop antennae were added in 1982, increasing the building's total height by 253 feet and serving the many broadcasting organizations based inside the tower.

Seeing for miles Although the audiovisual presentation on Chicago at ground level is uninspiring, the 103rd-floor Skydeck is not. Accessible via a 70-second elevator ride, it reveals a tremendous panorama of the city and its surroundings. In each direction, a recorded commentary describes the view and landmark buildings, seen here as few were ever intended to be seen: from above. Sears, the retail company that commissioned the building and used its lower floors, moved out in 1992. Note Alexander Calder's moving sculpture, *Universe*, in the lobby at the Wacker Drive entrance.

8

CHICAGO BOARD OF TRADE

An aluminum statue of Ceres, the Roman goddess of agriculture, looks down over the Loop's financial institutions from the top of the Chicago Board of Trade. Strikingly sited above La Salle Street, this building embodies what Chicago is about.

Order from chaos Founded in 1848, the Chicago Board of Trade (CBOT) brought order and organization to the previously chaotic system of grain trading, ending widely fluctuating prices and creating a stable market for the farm produce of the Midwest. Since 1930, the CBOT has occupied this eye-catching building, richly endowed with art-deco motifs and a profusion of polished marble and shiny chrome.

Speedy dealing Ideally, arrive in the fifth-floor visitors' gallery shortly before the 9:30AM commencement of trading, and acquaint yourself with the layout of the trading floor before the day's hectic events begin. Each of a series of octagonal open pits specializes in one commodity. Above the pits, the walls are lined by screens that flash the latest prices for wheat, corn, soybeans, and other produce. As trading commences, each pit becomes a flurry of activity. The traders here move an estimated $13 trillion across the floor each year.

DID YOU KNOW?

- Architects: Holabird & Root (1930), Murphy/Jahn (1983)
- Number of stories: 45
- Trading room height: six stories
- Trading floor size: 51,000sq feet
- Miles of telephone cable: 10,000
- Price changes displayed per day: 90,000
- Contracts exchanged annually: 13–14 million
- Ceres: sculpted by John H. Storrs
- Height of Ceres: 31 feet
- Height of Ceres above ground: 609 feet

INFORMATION

- ✚ G7
- ✉ 141 W. Jackson Boulevard
- ☎ 312/435–3500
- ◷ Visitor center: Mon–Fri 9–2. Closed holidays
- 🍴 Various restaurants and cafés
- Ⓜ Brown and Orange lines: Quincy
- 🚌 1, 60, 151
- ♿ Good
- 💲 Free
- ↔ Sears Tower (► 30), The Rookery (► 32), Carson Pirie Scott & Co. store (► 34)

Top: trading begins
Left: CBOT facade

THE ROOKERY

Designed by Daniel Burnham and John Wellborn Root in the 1880s, and later renovated by Frank Lloyd Wright, the Rookery is among Chicago's most admired and most influential landmarks.

Birdhouse After the Great Fire of 1871, birds took to roosting in the water-storage building that was temporarily City Hall. It was consequently nicknamed the Rookery. Public feeling dictated that the building that replaced it should formally take on this name. Rising 11 stories, the Rookery was among the tallest buildings in the world on completion and one of the most important early skyscrapers: the thick load-bearing brick and granite walls at the base, decorated with Roman, Moorish, and Venetian (and several rook) motifs, support upper levels with an iron frame that enabled the structure to be raised higher than previously thought possible.

Interior treasures The facade, however, is scant preparation for the interior. The inner court is bathed in incredible levels of natural light entering through a vast domed skylight. Imposing lamps hang above the floor, and Root's intricate ironwork decorates the stairways that climb up to a 360-degree balcony. The white marble, introduced by Frank Lloyd Wright in 1905, increases the sense of space and brightness.

CHICAGO HISTORICAL SOCIETY

Almost as old as the city itself, this institution not only has a fine collection of artifacts relating to the city's past but also is a world leader in studying U.S. history in general.

Chicago collections The society occupies a Georgian-style brick building constructed in 1932, with a modern, glass-walled extension. It is just inside Lincoln Park near the southwest entrance. Generations of Chicago schoolchildren have come here to learn about their city's history. From the Union Stockyards to the Chicago Bears, every major facet in Chicago's rise from swampland to metropolis is discussed and illustrated in the chronologically arranged galleries. A page from an 1833 *Daily News* debating the potential impact of the coming of railroads, the city's first locomotive, and a colorful array of vintage rail company posters demonstrate the city's role as a transportation center. A lively display describes the gangster era; elsewhere the Haymarket Riot and Pullman Strike are thoughtfully covered and placed in context as part of the growth of the city's blue-collar militancy. Other exhibits cogently outline the emergence of Chicago as a center of architectural innovation.

The American Wing Alongside temporary shows, the society's American Wing houses two exhibitions that explore U.S. history via informative texts and an excellent collection of period items. "We The People" charts the nation's growth from the fight for, and acquisition of, independence to the creation of the constitution and Westward Expansion. "A House Divided" focuses on the North–South conflicts in the young nation, looking particularly at the issue of slavery and the events leading to the Civil War.

HIGHLIGHTS

- *The Railsplitter*, painting of Abraham Lincoln
- Civil War surrender table
- John Brown's bible
- Abraham Lincoln's deathbed
- 1920s bootleg liquor still
- Mementoes from 1893 World's Fair
- Chicago's first fire engine
- Poignant Great Fire exhibits

INFORMATION

- ✚ G3
- ✉ 1601 N. Clark Street
- ☎ 312/642–4600
- 🕐 Mon–Sat 9:30–4:30; Sun noon–5
- 🍴 Big Shoulders Café
- 🚇 Brown line: Sedgwick
- 🚌 11, 22, 36, 72, 151, 156
- ♿ Good
- 💲 Inexpensive; free Mon
- ↔ Lincoln Park (➤ 29), International Museum of Surgical Sciences (➤ 38)

CARSON PIRIE SCOTT & CO. STORE

DID YOU KNOW?

- 1856 Louis Sullivan born in Boston
- 1871–1874 Studies architecture at MIT and École de Beaux-Arts in Paris
- 1875 Moves to Chicago
- 1881 Forms architectural practice of Adler & Sullivan with Dankmar Adler
- 1886 Commences building of Chicago's acclaimed Auditorium Building
- 1890 Getty tomb completed for Graceland Cemetery
- 1924 *Autobiography of an Idea* is published, including Sullivan's phrase "form follows function." In the same year, Sullivan dies impoverished

INFORMATION

Probably no other store in the world has a more elaborately decorated exterior than that of Carson Pirie Scott & Co., created by the phenomenally gifted and influential architect Louis Sullivan over a five-year period beginning in 1899.

Nature's art While Sullivan was a key figure in what became known as the Chicago School of Architecture, the group that after Chicago's Great Fire gave the city the earliest skyscrapers, it was for his finely realized ornamentation that he became best known. With the cast-iron embellishment of the Carson Pirie Scott & Co. store, Sullivan's pre-dilection for flowing yet geometric forms reached new levels of artistry. Nowhere are his skills better expressed than in the store's corner entrance on State and Madison streets, and around the store's first- and second-floor windows, the showpiece windows intended to display merchandise.

Light and space The more austere terra-cotta-clad upper levels express the steel form of the building. The large windows span the entire width between the steel supports: known as "Chicago windows," and made possible by the invention of plate glass, they accentuate the horizontal, maximize the amount of natural light reaching the interior, and strengthen the general sense of geometric cohesion. A 1979 renovation restored many of Sullivan's forgotten features.

WRIGLEY BUILDING

In a prime site on classy Michigan Avenue stands the 1920s Wrigley Building, an elegant monument to high-rise architecture and to the Chicago-based company that is still the world's major manufacturer of chewing gum.

Forever gleaming The Wrigley Building was partly modeled on the Giralda Tower in Seville, Spain, although the many ornamental features echo the French Renaissance. It is actually two structures rather than one. The North and South buildings stand behind a continuous facade linked by an arcaded walkway at ground level and by two enclosed aerial walkways. The ornate glazed terra-cotta facade has never been restored but has retained its original gleam. The effect is most pronounced at night, when banks of 1,000-watt bulbs illuminate the exterior.

Northern pioneer It is hard to believe today, but at the time of construction there were no office buildings north of the Loop. The Wrigley Building, raised at the same time as the Michigan Avenue Bridge, was always intended as the gateway to the city's so-called Near North neighborhoods. The building's offices were fully rented immediately after completion, and house public relations, advertising, and publishing companies.

DID YOU KNOW?

- Architects: Graham, Anderson, Probst & White
- Excavation begins: Jan 1920
- Completion: South Building—April 1921; North Building—May 1924
- Height: 425 feet
- Stories: South—30; North—21
- Area: 453,433sq feet
- Office workers employed in building: 1,300
- Clock-face diameter: 19 feet 7 inches
- Clock hour-hand length: 6 feet 4 inches
- Clock minute-hand length: 9 feet 2 inches

INFORMATION

- ✚ H5
- ✉ 400 N. Michigan Avenue
- ☎ 312/923–8080
- 🕐 Usual business hours
- Ⓟ Red line: Grand
- 🚌 3, 11, 29, 65, 147, 151, 157
- ♿ Good
- 🎫 Free
- ↔ Terra Museum of American Art (► 36), Tribune Tower (► 39), Museum of Contemporary Art (► 52), IBM Building (► 55)

TERRA MUSEUM OF AMERICAN ART

HIGHLIGHTS

- *The Jolly Flatboatman,*
  George Caleb Bingham
- *The Last of the Mohicans,*
  Thomas Cole
- *Our Banner in the Sky,*
  Frederick Church
- *The Checker Players,*
  Milton Avery
- *Brooklyn Bridge on the*
  River, Max Weber

INFORMATION

- H5
- 666 N. Michigan Avenue
- 312/664–3939
- Tue 10–6; Wed–Sat 10–5;
  Sun noon–5
- Red line: Grand
- 3, 11, 125, 145, 146, 147,
  151
- Moderate donation; free Tue
  and first Sun of month
- Wrigley Building (➤ 35),
  Tribune Tower (➤ 39),
  Museum of Contemporary
  Art (➤ 52), IBM Building
  (➤ 55)
- Free guided tours: Tue–Fri
  noon and 2PM weekends

Top: The Last of the
Mohicans *by Thomas*
Cole (1801–1848)

With temporary and long-term exhibitions of quality, the Terra Museum insightfully explores the development of art in the United States and the rise to international preeminence of some of the nation's artists.

Industrial art The Terra is a rarity among the nation's art museums in having been designed solely to display American art. The museum was created by wealthy industrialist-entrepreneur Daniel J. Terra—who built a fortune on fast-drying ink—to showcase his own collections. The museum also borrows works for the frequently outstanding temporary shows that highlight work by American artists who have been neglected or otherwise undervalued by mainstream art museums. Terra, who served as a cultural affairs ambassador in the Reagan administration, also opened a sister museum in Giverney, France, to display American works painted in that country. Inspired by New York's Guggenheim, the Terra's design includes ramps between floors so that you can start at the top level and wind your way down.

The galleries Following several Whistler etchings, the "Attitudes Towards Nature" gallery explores the changing face of the American landscape as depicted by its early painters, among them Thomas Cole (founder of the Hudson River School), Thomas Moran, and Frederick Church. Subsequent rooms display works by important figures such as William Homer and George Caleb Bingham, and lead into walls of moderns including pieces by Joseph Stella, Edward Hopper, and Milton Avery. A well-lit alcove is the setting for the "collection cameo," where a particular work is hung alongside a detailed accompanying text.

CHICAGO CULTURAL CENTER

Even in a city richly endowed with architectural marvels, the stunning, early 20th-century Chicago Cultural Center—nicknamed "the people's palace"—is a treasure. It houses free exhibits and the Museum of Broadcast Communications.

The exhibitions Completed in 1897 and serving as the city's main public library until 1974, the Chicago Cultural Center mounts displays that usually focus on aspects of Chicago history and architecture. Several exhibits run concurrently. The entertaining Museum of Broadcast Communications explores the history of American radio and TV with displays of vintage transmitting and receiving equipment, and recordings of historic broadcasts. Much more impressive to first-time visitors is the sheer grandeur of the building, with its gleaming marble, stained glass, and polished brass, all in beaux-arts style.

The architecture The Washington Street entrance leads visitors through hefty bronze doors set beneath a Romanesque portal into the main lobby, whose grand staircase is bordered by exquisite mosaics set into its white Carrara marble balustrades. A visitor information office occupies part of the second floor, while the third holds the Preston Bradley Hall, whose awe-inspiring 38-foot Tiffany-glass dome has been valued at $35 million. The main exhibition hall is on the next level, where gorgeously decorated columns rise to meet an immaculately coffered ceiling.

DID YOU KNOW?

- Architects: Holabird & Root (1897)
- Restoration: Shepley, Rutan & Coolridge (1977, 1993)
- Main exhibit space area: 7,600 feet
- Number of exhibit visitors: 600,000 annually

INFORMATION

- ✚ H6
- ✉ 78 E. Washington Street
- ☎ 312/629–6630
- 🕐 Mon–Wed 10–7; Thu 10–9; Fri 10–6; Sat 10–5; Sun noon–5
- 🍴 Café
- 🚇 Brown and Orange lines: Madison
- 🚌 3, 4, 60, 145, 147, 151
- ♿ Good
- 🎫 Free
- ↔ Carson Pirie Scott & Co. store (► 34), Art Institute of Chicago (► 40)
- ❓ Guided architectural tours: Tue, Wed, and Sat (☎ 312/744–6630)

15

MUSEUM OF SURGICAL SCIENCES

HIGHLIGHTS

- Professor W. T. Eckley's Dissecting Class (photo)
- Drilled Peruvian skulls
- 15th–16th-century amputation saw
- Needles and probes from Pompeii
- 1950s X-ray shoe-fitter
- Gallstone collection
- Civil War field amputation kit
- Reprint of Versalius's notebook
- Laennec's stethoscope

INFORMATION

- ✚ H3
- ✉ 1524 N. Lake Shore Drive
- ☎ 312/642–6502
- 🕐 Tue–Sat 10–4
- Ⓜ Brown line: Sedgwick
- 🚌 151
- ♿ Good
- 💵 Moderate donation
- ↔ Lincoln Park (➤ 29), Chicago Historical Society (➤ 33)

Ancient surgery: a drilled skull

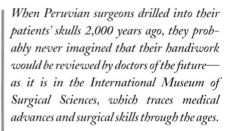

When Peruvian surgeons drilled into their patients' skulls 2,000 years ago, they probably never imagined that their handiwork would be reviewed by doctors of the future— as it is in the International Museum of Surgical Sciences, which traces medical advances and surgical skills through the ages.

House of health Founded in 1953, the museum is dedicated to enhancing the understanding of surgery past and present. It has several floors of exhibits, as well as innovative temporary shows covering diverse subjects related to health and medicine. The collection is housed in a stately mansion designed by celebrated Chicago architect Howard Van Doren Shaw and completed in 1917. A visit here not only informs on surgical matters but provides an insight into the domestic arrangements of a moneyed Chicago family of the early 20th century.

Tools of the trade Among the oldest exhibits are drilled skulls discovered in ancient Peruvian temples, surgeons' tools found in excavations at the Roman town of Pompeii, and ancestor skulls used by shamans of Papua New Guinea to frighten evil spirits. Pioneering surgeons from various countries are commemorated with somber portraits and, in one case, a bronze replica of the surgeon's right hand. Many rooms are packed with displays of fearsome needles, hooks, and other sharp metalic things used for all manner of gouging, probing, and extracting. Less unnerving are the early microscopes, the room filled with bulky X-ray machines, and the stethoscope of one Doctor Theophile Laennec, which was designed to be fitted inside a top hat.

TRIBUNE TOWER

In the 1920s, the **Chicago Tribune** *news-paper staged a competition for the design of its new premises. The competition attracted many leading architects, and the winning entry has become one of the most loved elements of this fashionable stretch of Michigan Avenue.*

Modern medieval Although Eliel Saarinen's second-placed entry came to wield greater influence on the future of high-rise building, it was the neo-gothic design by John Mead Howells and Raymond Hood that took the $100,000 first prize. Using vertical lines of differing width and a buttressed tower, Howells and Hood created a 46-story building that looks like an elongated medieval cathedral. The structure was completed in 1925.

Stone-studded The building is best admired from a distance, although the lobby displays two former *Tribune* front pages, one marking the Great Fire of 1871 and the other America's entry into World War I. You can watch WGN, the Tribune-owned radio station, through the studio's street-level window. Embedded in the building's walls are stones from the world's most famous landmark buildings, pilfered by *Tribune* foreign correspondents at the request of Robert McCormick, the paper's larger-than-life publisher for 45 years, from 1910 until his death in 1955.

DID YOU KNOW?

Tribune Tower includes stones from:
- The Berlin Wall, Germany
- The Alamo, Texas
- The Great Wall, China
- Westminster Abbey, London
- Notre Dame, Paris
- The Great Pyramid, Egypt
- St. Peter's, Rome
- The Colosseum, Rome
- Hans Christian Andersen's home, Denmark

INFORMATION

✚	H5
✉	435 N. Michigan Avenue
☎	312/222–9100
⏱	Normal business hours
Ⓜ	Red line: Grand
🚍	3, 11, 29, 65, 147, 151, 157
♿	Good
🎟	Free
↔	Wrigley Building (► 35), Terra Museum of American Art (► 36), Museum of Contemporary Art (► 52), IBM Building (► 55)

Top: a radio show in progress
Left: the Tribune Tower entrance

ART INSTITUTE OF CHICAGO

HIGHLIGHTS

- *Time Transfixed*, Magritte
- *Personages with Stars*, Miró
- *Improvization 30 (Cannons)*, Kandinsky
- *Mother and Child*, Picasso
- *Two Sisters (on the Terrace)*, Renoir
- *Bedroom at Arles*, Van Gogh
- The Arthur Rubloff Paperweight Collection

INFORMATION

- ✚ H7
- ✉ 111 S. Michigan Avenue
- ☎ 312/443–3600
- 🕐 Mon, Wed–Fri 10:30–4:30; Tue 10:30–8; Sat 10–5; Sun noon–5
- 🍴 Café
- 🚇 Brown and Orange lines: Adams
- 🚌 3, 4, 60, 145, 147, 151
- ♿ Good
- 💲 Moderate; free on Tue
- ↔ Carson Pirie Scott & Co. store (➤ 34), Chicago Cultural Center (➤ 37), Grant Park (➤ 41)
- ❓ Free tours daily

Housed in a classically inspired building erected for the World's Columbian Exposition (1893), the Art Institute has an acclaimed collection of Impressionist paintings. But its galleries showcase much more, from arms and armor to the original trading room of the Stock Exchange.

Masterworks Except for the celebrated *American Gothic* by Grant Wood, which is displayed amid the American collections, the pick of the paintings is the European art grouped chronologically around the second floor. No

work receives greater notice and admiration than Seurat's expansive *A Sunday Afternoon on the Island of La Grande Jatte*, a pointillist masterpiece. Seminal works in adjacent galleries include haystacks by Monet, dancers by Degas, a self-portrait on cardboard by Van Gogh, and the vibrant *Paris Street, Rainy Day* by the less well-known Caillebotte. Among the many striking modern works are Picasso's *The Old Guitarist* and Hopper's moody *Nighthawks*.

Curiosities Everything from Chinese ceramics to Guatemalan textiles has a niche on the first floor. There is a huge collection of paperweights, and there are swords, daggers, and chain mail. Leave time for the stunning 1898 Trading Room of the Chicago Stock Exchange, designed by Louis Sullivan and reconstructed here.

Above: Grant Wood's American Gothic

GRANT PARK

Planned by Daniel Burnham in 1909 as the centerpiece of a series of lakefront parks, Grant Park is a major festival venue that in its past has seen everything from an infamous violence-marred 1968 anti-Vietnam War demonstration to a 1979 papal mass.

City views Far from being a bucolic extravaganza, Grant Park is essentially a succession of lawns crisscrossed by walkways and split in two by busy Lake Shore Drive. Bordered by the high-rises of the Loop and the expanses of Lake Michigan, Grant Park never lets you forget that you are in Chicago. Its Petrillo Music Shell provides a hospitable setting for summer concerts.

Buildings banished A section of today's park was designated as public land in 1836, but it reached its present size by expanding on to rubble from the 1871 fire, dumped as landfill in Lake Michigan. Its prime commercial location made Grant Park a target for developers, and only the energy and finances of Chicago-based mail-order pioneer A. Montgomery Ward, who engaged in a series of court battles, kept buildings from going up on its 319 acres. Among the features is the 1926 Buckingham Fountain, notable for its computer-choreographed display of colored lights dancing on the 1.5 million gallons of water that are pumped daily.

Events Grant Park is the venue for the city's most popular open-air events that attract millions of visitors every year, including blues, jazz, and gospel music festivals, classical music concerts, and the well-attended Taste of Chicago—for 11 days leading up to July 4 more than 70 local restaurants set up tents along the sidewalk to sell their gastronomical creations.

HIGHLIGHTS

- Blues Festival (June)
- Gospel Festival (June)
- Taste of Chicago (June–July)
- Independence Day concert and firework display (July)
- Jazz Festival (September)

INFORMATION

- ✚ H/J6/7/8/9
- ✉ Bordered by N. Michigan Avenue, E. Randolph Drive, Roosevelt Drive, and Lake Michigan
- ☎ Petrillo Music Shell concert information: 312/742–4763
- ◷ Visit during daylight hours only, except for special evening events
- Ⓢ Brown and Orange lines: Randolph, Madison, or Adams
- ▥ 3, 4, 6, 38, 60, 145, 146, 147, 151, 157
- ♿ Good
- Ⓕ Free
- ⟷ Carson Pirie Scott & Co. store (➤ 34), Chicago Cultural Center (➤ 37), Art Institute of Chicago (➤ 40), Field Museum of Natural History (➤ 42), John G. Shedd Aquarium (➤ 44), Adler Planetarium & Astronomy Museum (➤ 46)

FIELD MUSEUM OF NATURAL HISTORY

HIGHLIGHTS

- Sue
- "Traveling the Pacific"
- Stuffed gorilla
- Gem collection
- Pawnee earth lodge
- Tibet collections

INFORMATION

- ✚ H/J8
- ✉ E. Roosevelt Road at Lake Shore Drive
- ☎ 312/922–9410
- ⏱ Daily 9–5
- 🍴 Coffee shop; McDonald's
- Ⓜ Orange line: Roosevelt
- 🚉 Roosevelt Road
- 🚌 146
- ♿ Good
- 🎫 Moderate; free Wed
- ↔ Grant Park (➤ 41), John G. Shedd Aquarium (➤ 44), Adler Planetarium (➤ 46)

An impressive exhibit in the dinosaur section

One of the world's great natural history museums, the Field displays superb exhibits drawn from all corners of the globe. After a strenuous round of viewing, ponder the fact that only around one percent of the museum's 20 million artifacts is on display.

The building The museum was completed in 1920, its cavernous galleries providing a home for a collection originally assembled for Chicago's 1893 World's Columbian Exposition. With its porticoes, columns, and beaux-arts decoration, the imposing design sits rather uneasily with the needs of a modern museum, and sometimes the many rooms of exhibits from myriad eras and cultures can make for difficult viewing. Nonetheless, steady upgrading and innovative ideas in layout have made certain parts of the museum a rip-roaring success.

Great exhibits The outstanding sections include the dinosaur exhibits in which Sue, the most complete Tyrannosaurus rex ever found, takes pride of place; major ancient Egyptian artifacts, spanning 5000 BC to AD 300, arranged in and around the dimly lit and labyrinthine innards of a life-size re-created tomb of a 5th-dynasty pharaoh; and "Traveling the Pacific," a powerful examination of cultural and spiritual life in Pacific cultures and the threats posed by the Western world's encroachment. Also noteworthy are the Native American displays and the sparkling gem collection, which includes pieces purchased in the 1890s from the famous Tiffany & Co. jewelers.

GLESSNER HOUSE MUSEUM

This home of a farm-machinery mogul, the only surviving example of the work of architect H.H. Richardson, profoundly influenced American domestic architecture and inspired future designers such as Louis Sullivan. It is a beautiful house, and still in beautiful shape.

Outside structure In 1885 a leading Chicago couple, John and Frances Glessner, commissioned Boston architect Henry Hobson Richardson to design a home for them. In contrast to the European revival-style homes dominating what was then Chicago's most fashionable neighborhood, the Glessners' house was given a fortress-like stone facade, and an L-shape that enabled its main rooms to face not the street, as was the vogue, but an inner courtyard. Initially, neighbors found the house objectionable, but many revised their opinions once invited in.

The Glessners' home In the house, oak beams and panels exude a warmth, and clever planning has created subtle distinctions between public areas and private ones. Richardson designed many furnishings, including the large oak desk in the library which, significantly for the time, was intended as a workplace for Mrs Glessner as well as for her husband. The Glessners' personal appreciation of art and design is reflected by their use of William Morris tiles and wall coverings, and the Isaac Scott ceramics and cabinets. John Glessner's photographs, which are on display in the house, confirm that the present-day appearance of the house and its furnishings is much the same as that enjoyed by the Glessners until their deaths in the 1930s. Rescued in 1966, Glessner House is now a National Historic Landmark.

DID YOU KNOW

- 1838 Henry Hobson Richardson born in Louisiana
- 1859 Becomes the second American to study at the École de Beaux-Arts in Paris
- 1873 Establishes a reputation with the Romanesque-style church in Boston
- 1886 Dies just prior to the completion of the Glessner House

INFORMATION

- H9
- 1800 S. Prairie Avenue
- 312/326–1480
- Guided tours: Wed–Sun 1, 2, 3
- Red line: Cermak/Chinatown
- 1, 18, 38
- Few
- Moderate
- Clarke House (➤ 54)

JOHN G. SHEDD AQUARIUM

HIGHLIGHTS

- Pacific white-sided dolphins
- Beluga whales
- Sea otters
- Sea anemones
- Penguins
- Turtles

INFORMATION

- ✛ J8
- ✉ 1200 S. Lake Shore Drive
- ☎ 312/939–2438
- ⏰ Daily 9–5; Memorial Day–Labor Day 9–6.
- 🍴 Soundings Restaurant; snacks from various stands at Bubble Net Food Court
- Ⓖ Orange line: Roosevelt
- 🚉 Roosevelt Road
- 🚌 146
- ♿ Excellent
- 💲 Expensive. Aquarium free Thu; other exhibits reduced fee
- ↔ Grant Park (➤ 41), Field Museum (➤ 42), Adler Planetarium (➤ 46)

Chicago's "Ocean-by-the-Lake" is the world's largest indoor aquarium, enhanced by the addition of a state-of-the-art oceanarium where you can watch dolphins and whales show off typical behaviors.

Aquarium A re-created Caribbean coral reef at the center of this imposing Greek-style building is home to barracuda, moray eels, nurse sharks, and other creatures, who are fed several times daily by a team of microphone-equipped divers who describe the creatures, their habits, and their habitat. Around the reef, denizens of the deep waters of the world occupy geographically arranged tanks. Look for the false-eye flashlight fish, born with the piscine equivalent of a flashlight; the mimic roundhead, able to deter predators by making its lower half resemble a moray eel; and the matamata turtle, so sluggish that you'll be lucky to see it move.

Oceanarium Dolphins and whales are the star attractions here. Five times daily, the dolphins display natural skills such as "spy-hopping," when a dolphin raises itself onto its tail to an audience seated around a re-created chunk of Pacific Northwest coast. Winding nature trails lead to the lower-level windows that provide an underwater view of the dolphins and whales. You also see a colony of penguins, and hands-on exhibits that describe facets of sea-mammal life, such as underwater movement, respiratory system, diet, mating habits, and interaction with other sea creatures.

Decorations on the aquarium door illustrate the sea life within

DU SABLE MUSEUM

One of the unsung museums of Chicago, this one chronicles aspects of black history, chiefly focusing on African–Americans but also encompassing African and Caribbean cultures.

Settlers The museum is named after Chicago's first permanent settler, Jean-Baptiste Point du Sable, a Haitian trader born of a French father and African slave mother. Further African-American arrivals came in three main waves—during the late 19th century and during the two World Wars—settling mostly on Chicago's South Side. Black businesses became established, while the expanding community provided the voter base for the first blacks to enter Chicago politics. Among the settlers were many musicians, and what became Chicago blues was born—an electrified urban form of rural blues fused with elements of jazz. The turbulent 1960s saw growing radicalism among Chicago's African-Americans, and the beginning of the rise to national prominence of South Side's Jesse Jackson.

Part of the display of African sculpture

Exhibits The first-floor rooms display items from the permanent collection, but there are also meticulously planned temporary exhibitions, which in the past have featured the sacred art of Ethiopia and celebrated the life and music of Duke Ellington.

DID YOU KNOW?

- 1850 Passing of Illinois' Fugitive Slave Law makes Chicago an important stop on the "Underground Railroad" of escaped slaves
- 1871 First Chicago black elected to public office
- 1900 Chicago's black population: 31,150
- 1905 Founding of the nationally influential African-American-run newspaper, *Chicago Defender*
- 1919 What newspapers call a race riot leaves 38 dead
- 1940 Chicago's black population: 278,000
- 1950 Chicago's black population: 492,000
- 1968 Jesse Jackson founds PUSH on South Side
- 1983 Harold Washington is elected Chicago's first black mayor

INFORMATION

- ✚ Off map to south
- ✉ 740 E. 56th Place
- ☎ 773/947–0600
- 🕐 Mon–Sat 10–5; Sun noon–5
- Ⓡ Red line: Garfield
- 🚏 59th Street
- 🚍 4
- ♿ Good
- 🎫 Inexpensive; free on Thu
- ↔ Oriental Institute (➤ 47), Museum of Science and Industry (➤ 48)

ADLER PLANETARIUM

HIGHLIGHTS

- Sky Show
- Apache Point Observing Station link-up
- Space Transporters
- Martian rocks
- Voyager images of Saturn

INFORMATION

- J8
- 1300 S. Lake Shore Drive
- 312/322–0304
- June–Labor Day: Mon–Wed 9–5; Thu–Fri 9–9; Sat–Sun 9–6. Rest of year: daily 9–6
- Cafeteria
- Orange line: Roosevelt
- Roosevelt Road
- 146
- Good
- Inexpensive; free entry to building on Tue
- Grant Park (➤ 41), Field Museum (➤ 42), John G. Shedd Aquarium (➤ 44)

Bringing close-up views of deep space to Chicagoans and other earthlings, the Friday evening Sky Show has helped the Adler Planetarium and Astronomy Museum to win local hearts since it opened in 1930.

Skywatching Max Adler, a Sears Roebuck executive, realized his ambition to put the wonders of the cosmos within the reach of ordinary people when he provided the money to have the western hemisphere's first modern planetarium built in Chicago. The planetarium's floors, corridors, and stairways hold one of the world's major astronomical collections. The landmark building is a dodecahedron in rainbow granite, decorated by signs of the zodiac and topped by a lead-covered copper dome. The fascinating hour-long Sky Show examines themes in astronomy, first using a multimedia theater and then the 68-foot dome of the Sky Theater. On Friday evenings the Sky Show displays live images from the observatory's own 20-inch computer-controlled telescope.

Finding space The museum's collections are thematically arranged on three floors linked by stairways showing deep-space photographs. An extraordinary collection of astrolabes and other items portrays the astronomy of the Middle Ages. Navigation and the development of telescopes are the main theme on the second floor, where pride of place goes to the exhibit on Sir William Herschel, the musician-turned-astronomer who discovered Uranus in 1781. The first floor gets to grips with space exploration, displaying an Apollo space suit and samples of Martian rock.

ORIENTAL INSTITUTE

The University of Chicago's Oriental Institute is a leader among museums and research centers specializing in the Middle East. The sheer volume of exhibits creates a powerful impression of ancient cultures.

The history In the 1890s, the newly founded University of Chicago was already showing off a modest collection of Middle East antiquities. As the university embarked on its own field trips the collections expanded significantly, and in 1919 the Oriental Institute was established. Since then, the institute's finds, and its acclaimed interpretation of them, have greatly enhanced the understanding and appreciation of the once mighty kingdoms of Egypt, Assyria, Anatolia, Mesopotamia, and neighboring regions. The museum was purpose-built in 1931 by the firm of Mayers, Murray & Phillips, who included numerous Middle Eastern motifs. A major renovation during the 1990s restored many original architectural features.

The galleries Amid the mummy masks, royal seals, and polished clay pots, several sizable pieces stand out. Dominating the Egyptian section is an enormous statue of Tutankhamun, from his tomb in the Valley of Kings. In the Assyrian section is the human-headed winged bull, an immense sculpture that once stood in the palace of the powerful Sargon II (reigned 721–705 BC). Also from Sargon II's palace is a stone relief showing two officials. The museum's whole collection—so extensive that only a small fraction can be displayed at one time—spans about 3,000 years, from the 2nd millennium BC.

HIGHLIGHTS

- Tutankhamun statue
- Human-headed winged bull
- Relief from the tomb of Mentuemhat
- Striding lion
- Clay prism of Sennacherib
- Egyptian Book of the Dead
- Archaic-period bed
- Statue of Horus
- Mesopotamian four-faced god and goddess

INFORMATION

- 🔲 Off map to south
- ✉ 1155 E. 58th Street
- ☎ 312/702–9520
- 🕐 Tue, Thu–Sat 10–4; Wed 10–8:30; Sun noon–4
- Ⓡ Red line: Garfield
- 🚉 59th Street
- 🚌 4, 55
- ♿ Good
- 🎫 Free
- ↔ Du Sable Museum of African-American History (▶ 45), Museum of Science and Industry (▶ 48)

Top: Sumerian votive statues
Left: a sandstone statue of Tutankhamun

47

25

MUSEUM OF SCIENCE & INDUSTRY

HIGHLIGHTS

- AIDS exhibit
- "Take Flight"
- Apollo 8
- Space Shuttle
- Simulated F-14 mission
- Piccard Stratosphere Glider
- Re-created coal mine
- Heart
- "Managing Urban Wastes" exhibit

INFORMATION

- ✚ Off map to south
- ✉ 57th Street at Lake Shore Drive
- ☎ 312/684–1414
- ◑ Summer: daily 9:30–5:30. Rest of the year: Mon–Fri 9:30–4; Sat–Sun 9:30–5:30
- 🍴 Several cafés
- Ⓡ Red line: Garfield
- ▮ 55th, 56th, 57th Street
- ▭ 6, 10
- ♿ Excellent
- 🎫 Moderate; free on Thu; separate charge for Omnimax Theater
- ↔ Du Sable Museum of African-American History (► 45), Oriental Institute (► 47)

With 2,000 exhibits spread across 15 acres, the Museum of Science and Industry easily fills a day. Even know–it–all visitors find hours passing like minutes as they discover new things about the world —and beyond it—at every turn.

Flying high The first eye-catching item is a Boeing 727 attached to an interior balcony. Packed with multimedia exhibits, the plane simulates a flight from San Francisco to Chicago, making full use of flaps, rudders, and undercarriage, all fully explained. Other flight-related exhibits include a simulated mission aboard a naval F-14 fighter. Reflecting other modes of transportation are the 500mph Spirit of America car, a walk-through 1944 German U-boat, and the Apollo 8 spacecraft. The moon-circling Apollo craft forms just a small part of the excellent Henry Crown Space Center, housed in an adjoining building.

Medical matters A 16-foot-high walk-through heart sits among exhibits detailing the workings of the human body. Close by, in the AIDS exhibit, imaginative devices explain much about viruses and the workings of the immune system. The display has a computer-generated voyage into the body, which illustrates the attack strategy of the HIV virus and the approaches used by scientists to combat it.

CHICAGO's *best*

NEIGHBORHOODS

CHINATOWN

Other Chinese enclaves exist in Chicago, but the longest-established area—and what the city thinks of as Chinatown—is the eight blocks around the junction of Wentworth Avenue and Cermak Road, south of downtown. Packed with restaurants and bakeries, herbalists and tea shops, Chinatown resounds to the snap of firecrackers each February during Chinese New Year, one of Chicago's liveliest festivals.

✚ G9/10 🚇 Red line: Cermak/Chinatown 🚌 24

One of many busy restaurants in Chinatown

HYDE PARK AND KENWOOD

Between Hyde Park Boulevard and the University of Chicago campus, Hyde Park became established, from the 1880s, as a leafy suburb complete with two parks designed by Frederick Law Olmsted and Calvert Vaux. Many early homes have been demolished, but some remain in Kenwood, north of Hyde Park Boulevard. Both areas are now populated predominantly by professionals, and have numerous bookstores and restaurants.

✚ Off map to south 🚇 Red line: Garfield 🚌 Hyde Park-53rd 🚌 1, 4, 28, 51

THE LOOP

So-named for its position within the loop formed by the El, the Loop is Chicago's business district and the home of the city's most celebrated architecture. The Loop is the vibrant hub of the city by day—virtually deserted by night.

✚ G/H6/7 🚇 All El lines converge on the Loop 🚌 Most north–south routes.

The Gold Coast

In the late 19th century, a top Chicago businessman astonished his peers by erecting a mansion home on undeveloped land well north of the Loop close to Lake Michigan. As others followed, the area became known as the Gold Coast, its streets lined by the elegant townhouses of the city's well-to-do. Many of the homes remain, joined by ultra-luxurious apartment towers.

✚ H3/4

MAGNIFICENT MILE

The favored shopping strip for wealthy Chicagoans, the section of Michigan Avenue between the Chicago River and Oak Street was named the Magnificent Mile by a property developer in the 1940s. The street's elegant stores, gleaming high-rise shopping malls, and designer outlets pay some of the city's highest commercial rents.

🔴 H4/5 🚇 Red line: Grand, Chicago 🚌 3, 11, 125, 145, 146, 147, 151

OAK PARK

From 1889, Frank Lloyd Wright added some 25 buildings in his evolving Prairie School style to the Victorian homes along the tree-lined streets of Oak Park, 8 miles west of the Loop. Ernest Hemingway (► 53) called it a town of "broad lawns and narrow minds."

🔴 Off map to west 🚇 Metra Line West 🚉 Oak Park 🚌 23

PRINTER'S ROW

The industrial buildings lining Dearborn Street, which runs south from the Loop, were the center of Chicago's printing industry during the late 19th century. Many are now loft-style apartments, with galleries and restaurants.

🔴 G7 🚇 Blue line: La Salle; Red line: Harrison 🚌 22, 62

RIVER NORTH

In the angle formed by the two branches of the Chicago River north of the Loop, this area of handsome warehouses is now filled with commercial art galleries, auction houses, eateries, and nightspots.

🔴 G/H5/6 🚇 Brown line: Chicago; Red line: Grand, Chicago 🚌 22, 37, 41, 65, 66

UKRAINIAN VILLAGE

Ukrainians settled this area off W. Chicago Avenue during the early 1900s. Evidence of the old country includes St. Nicholas Cathedral (► 56), Ukrainian eateries and stores, a culture center, and Ukrainian Independence Day festivities on January 22.

🔴 C5 🚇 Blue line: Chicago 🚌 66

A book market in full swing in Printer's Row

Wicker Park and Bucktown

The 4-acre park on Damen Avenue that gives Wicker Park its name is enclosed by gray-stone mansions. These days Wicker Park and neighboring Bucktown (north of Milwaukee Avenue) are fashionably bohemian, and known for their alternative music clubs and coffee bars that regularly stage poetry readings and performance art events.

🔴 C/D3/4

A Printer's Row mural illustrates the area's past

MUSEUMS

American Police Center & Museum

Grainy photos of Chicago cops through the decades, and displays on the 1886 Haymarket Riot and the 1968 Democratic Convention are among the exhibits at this barn-like museum. Other sections detail Chicago's gangster era and the capture in the city of John Dillinger. A wooden electric chair, believed to have been used during the 1920s, is also on view.

✉ 1717 S. State Street

BALZEKAS MUSEUM OF LITHUANIAN CULTURE
Regional folk costumes and other Lithuanian historical items form part of an extensive and absorbing collection.

✚ Off map to south ✉ 6500 S. Pulaski Road ☎ 773/582–6500 🕐 Daily 10–4 🚇 Orange line: Midway 🚌 53A ♿ Few 💲 Inexpensive

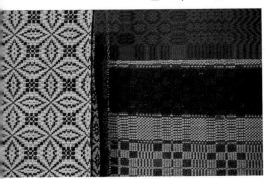

Display of textiles in the Balzekas Museum of Lithuanian Culture

MUSEUM OF CONTEMPORARY ART
Highlights from the permanent collection include the works of the Chicago-based Ed Paschke, and Richard Long's *Chicago Mud Circle* (1996), created directly on a gallery wall. The lower levels house temporary exhibitions and provide access to the Sculpture Garden.

✚ H5 ✉ 220 E. Chicago Avenue ☎ 312/280–2660 🕐 Tue 10–8; Wed–Sun 10–5 🚇 Red line: Chicago 🚌 157 ♿ Good 💲 Moderate; free on first Tue of month

MUSEUM OF CONTEMPORARY PHOTOGRAPHY
In addition to the museum's collection of American photography, you will find varied temporary exhibitions of contemporary photography from around the world.

✚ H7 ✉ 600 S. Michigan Avenue ☎ 312/663–5554 🕐 Mon–Fri 10–5; Sat noon–5 🚇 Red line: Harrison 🚌 1, 3, 4, 6, 38, 146 ♿ Good 💲 Free

ERNEST HEMINGWAY MUSEUM

A collection remembering the Nobel Prize-winning writer who spent his first 18 years in Oak Park. Open the same hours and on the the same street, at number 339 N., is Hemingway's birthplace.

✚ Off map to west ✉ 200 N. Oak Park Avenue ☎ 708/848–2222 🕐 Fri and Sun 1–5; Sat 10–5. Closed Mon–Thu 🚇 Green line: Harlem 🚉 Oak Park 🚌 23 ♿ Few 💲 Inexpensive

DAVID AND ALFRED SMART MUSEUM OF ART

An eclectic collection, with works by Auguste Rodin, Albrecht Dürer, and Mark Rothko, and furniture from Frank Lloyd Wright.

✚ Off map to south ✉ 5550 S. Greenwood Avenue ☎ 312/702–0200 🕐 Tue–Fri 10–4 (Thu until 9); Sat–Sun noon–6 🚇 Red line: Garfield 🚉 59th Street 🚌 4 ♿ Good 💲 Donations

SPERTUS MUSEUM OF JUDAICA

Torah scrolls, Hanukkah lamps, and tools used in circumcision are among the decorative and religious objects spanning 5,000 years that form the core of this museum's extensive collection of Judaica. However, only a small selection can be shown at any one time. The richness of most exhibits contrasts strongly with the somber collection of Holocaust memorabilia.

✚ H7 ✉ 618 S. Michigan Avenue ☎ 312/322–1747 🕐 Sun–Wed 10–5; Thu 10–8; Fri 10–3 🚇 Red line: Harrison 🚌 1, 3, 4, 6, 38, 146 ♿ Good 💲 Inexpensive; free Fri

National Vietnam Veteran's Art Museum

Paintings, sculpture, writing, and photography from (mostly) American combatants in Vietnam fill this museum. Adding to the sense of despair evoked by many works are the guns and equipment, used by both sides, that share the gallery space. The effect can be harrowing; one reviewer called the collection "art in a state of shock."

✉ 1801 S. Indiana Avenue

An exhibit from the Spertus Museum

HISTORIC BUILDINGS

Marquette Building

Completed in 1895, the Marquette Building is among the unsung masterpieces of Chicago architecture. It demonstrates the first use of the three-part "Chicago window"—plate glass spans the whole width between the building's steel supports. Lobby reliefs record the expedition of French Jesuit missionary Jacques Marquette; the entrance doors' panther heads are by Edward Kemeys, who is also responsible for the lions fronting the Art Institute of Chicago (➤ 40).
✉ 140 S. Dearborn Street

CLARKE HOUSE (1830s)

The Clarke House (named after its original owner) is the oldest structure in Chicago. The interior has been restored to a mid-19th-century appearance.
✚ H9 ✉ 1800 S. Prairie Avenue ☎ 312/326–1480 ⏰ Guided tours: Wed–Sun noon, 1, 2. Guided tours including Glessner House: Fri noon; Sat–Sun noon, 1, 2, 3 🚇 Red line: Cermak/Chinatown 🚉 18th Street 🚌 1, 3, 4, 18 ♿ Few 🎫 Moderate; can be combined with Glessner House

HISTORIC WATER TOWER (1869)

This pseudo-Gothic confection in yellow limestone, by William Boyington, is a city landmark.
✚ H5 ✉ 800 N. Michigan Avenue ☎ Ground-floor photography gallery 312/744–2400 ⏰ Mon–Sat 10–6:30; Sun 10–5 🚇 Red line: Chicago 🚌 11, 66, 145, 146, 147, 151 ♿ Few 🎫 Free

RELIANCE BUILDING (1895)

Charles Atwood preempted the modern skyscraper with this building's steel skeleton and large bay windows divided by slim terra-cotta mullions.
✚ H6 ✉ 32 N. State Street 🚇 Red or Blue lines: Washington 🚌 20, 22, 36, 56

ROBIE HOUSE (1910)

A famed example of Frank Lloyd Wright's Prairie School style of architecture. The horizontal emphasis reflects the Midwest's open spaces.
✚ Off map to south
✉ 5757 S. Woodlawn Avenue
☎ 708/848–1976
⏰ Guided tours: Mon–Fri 11, 1, 3. Continuous tours: Sat–Sun 11–3:30 🚇 Green Line: Cottage Grove 🚉 59th Street 🚌 4 ♿ Few 🎫 Free

The Historic Water Tower

MODERN BUILDINGS

See Top 25 Sights for
SEARS TOWER (▶ 30)

IBM BUILDING (1971)

The 54 stories of Mies van der Rohe's last office building rise sleekly above the Chicago River. His bust is in the lobby.

➕ H6 ✉ 330 N. Wabash Drive 🚇 Red line: Grand 🚌 29 ♿ Good

JAMES R. THOMPSON CENTER (1985)

This glass and steel edifice was designed by Helmut Jahn. Inside, a soaring atrium is lined with stores, restaurants, and cafés; upper levels house state agencies.

➕ G6 ✉ 100 W. Randolph Street ☎ 312/814–2141 🚇 Blue, Brown, Orange lines: Clark/Lake 🚌 156 ♿ Good

James R. Thompson Center's massive atrium

JOHN HANCOCK CENTER (1970)

The tapering profile of the John Hancock Center, designed by Skidmore, Owings & Merrill, is a feature of Chicago's skyline; until 1974, when Sears Tower was completed, it was the world's tallest building. It has an observatory (▶ 58).

➕ H4 ✉ 875 N. Michigan Avenue ☎ 312/751–3680 🏢 Skydeck Observatory: daily 9AM–midnight 🚇 Red line: Chicago 🚌 145, 146, 147, 151 ♿ Good 🎫 Skydeck Observatory: moderate

RICHARD J. DALEY CENTER (1965)

Jacques Brownson (of C. F. Murphy Associates) is credited with the center's design. Chiefly notable are the lobby's eternal flame memorial to the former mayor after whom the building is named, and the plaza's perplexing, untitled 1967 Picasso sculpture.

➕ G6 ✉ 50 W. Washington Street 🚇 Blue line: Washington 🚌 6, 11, 20, 23, 56 ♿ Good

333 W. WACKER DRIVE (1983)

The New York firm of Kohn Pedersen Fox struck a blow for postmodernism in Chicago with this acclaimed 36-story building, slotted ingeniously into a triangular site next to the river.

➕ G6 ✉ 333 W. Wacker Drive 🚇 Blue, Brown, Orange lines: Clark/Lake 🚌 16, 41, 125

Mies van der Rohe in Chicago

German-born Ludwig Mies van der Rohe, father of the International Style of architecture and one-time director of the German design school known as the Bauhaus, settled in Chicago in the 1940s, teaching at the Illinois Institute of Technology and redesigning it at the same time. Aside from the IBM Building and the institute, his most celebrated Chicago works are the glass and steel apartment buildings at 860–880 N. Lake Shore Drive.

55

PLACES OF WORSHIP

Holy Name Cathedral

See Excursions for
BAHA'I HOUSE OF WORSHIP (➤ 20)

FOURTH PRESBYTERIAN CHURCH (1914)
This Gothic Revival church serves a congregation drawn from Chicago's moneyed élite. Occasional but enjoyable lunchtime concerts pack the pews.

➕ H4 ✉ 126 E. Chestnut Street
☎ 312/787–2729 🚇 Red line: Chicago
🚌 145, 146, 147, 151 ♿ Good

HOLY NAME CATHEDRAL (1878)
The atmospheric seat of the Catholic Archdiocese of Chicago. In 1926, gangster and former choirboy "Hymie" Weiss was machine-gunned to death on the steps.

➕ H5 ✉ 735 N. State Street
☎ 312/787–8040 🚇 Red line: Chicago
🚌 29, 36 ♿ Good

ST. NICHOLAS CATHEDRAL (1915)
A Byzantine-style cathedral, modeled on the Basilica of St. Sophia in Kiev, and serving Chicago Ukrainians. The cathedral adopted the Gregorian calendar only in 1969, and then amid great opposition.

➕ C5 ✉ Junction of N. Oakley Boulevard and W. Rice Street ☎ 312/276–4537
🚇 Blue line: Chicago 🚌 66 ♿ Few

Quigley Seminary and St. James Chapel

An array of Gothic buildings, complete with leering gargoyles, lines a courtyard on Rush Street—west of the Magnificent Mile, between E. Chestnut and E. Pearson streets. Completed in the mid-1920s, the complex forms the Quigley Seminary and includes the St. James Chapel, decorated with stained-glass windows.

ST. STANISLAUS KOSTKA CHURCH (1881)
Raised to serve Chicago's Polish immigrants, this Renaissance-style church, modeled after a church in Krakow, Poland, quickly established the world's largest Catholic congregation.

➕ B4 ✉ 1351 W. Evergreen Avenue ☎ 773/278–2430 🚇 Blue line: Damen 🚌 52 ♿ Few

UNITY TEMPLE (1905)
Working to a tight budget, Frank Lloyd Wright used undecorated, reinforced concrete blocks—assembled into a series of interlocking sections—to create this temple for a Unitarian congregation in Oak Park. The furniture that Wright also designed for the building is still in use.

➕ Off map to west ✉ 875 Lake Street, Oak Park
☎ 708/383–8873 🕐 Mon–Fri 10–5. Guided tours on weekends
🚇 Blue line: Harlem 🚉 Oak Park 🚌 23 ♿ Few

PARKS, GARDENS & BEACHES

See Top 25 Sights for
GRANT PARK (➤ 41)
LINCOLN PARK (➤ 29)

JACKSON PARK

In 1893, 27 million people attended the World's Columbian Exposition, held in what became Jackson Park, now a pleasant green space with sports courts, a Japanese garden, and the Museum of Science and Industry (➤ 48).

✚ Off map to south ✉ Between S. Stony Island Avenue and Lake Michigan 🚇 Red line: Garfield 🚆 55th, 56th, 57th Street 🚌 6, 10

NORTH AVENUE BEACH

The mile-long North Avenue Beach draws a cross-section of the city's population, and is ideal for lazy sunbathing. Volleyball nets are provided, and there is a 1950s chess pavilion at the southern end of the beach.

✚ G/H1–3 ✉ Accessed from Lincoln Park 🚌 145, 146, 147, 151, 156

OAK PARK CONSERVATORY

Waterfalls, a herb garden, and assorted desert and tropical vegetation are among the highlights of this undervisited place.

✚ Off map to west ✉ 615 Garfield Street, Oak Park 🚇 Blue line: Oak Park Avenue 🚆 Oak Park 🚌 23

OAK STREET BEACH

The closeness of the exclusive Gold Coast neighborhood helps make Oak Street Beach the gathering place for some of Chicago's richest and best-toned bodies.

✚ H4 ✉ Access from junction of N. Michigan Avenue and E. Lake Shore Drive 🚌 145, 146, 147, 151

WASHINGTON SQUARE

This was Chicago's first public park, and once buzzed with Sunday after-noon soap-box orators. Lunching office workers and shoppers are now its main users.

✚ G4 ✉ Bordered by W. Walton Street and Delaware Place, and N. Clark and N. Dearborn streets 🚇 Red line: Chicago 🚌 22

Garfield Park Conservatory

Providing a refuge from urban Chicago, the conservatory has 5 acres of tropical and subtropical plants, and is open daily 9–5, all year round. The highlights include extensive collections of palms, ferns, and cacti. Chicagoans come here for expert gardening tips and for shows, when the opening hours are extended.

✉ 300 N. Central Park Boulevard

A sweeping view of the Chicago beaches

VIEWS

See Top 25 Sights for
SKYDECK, SEARS TOWER (▶ 30)

BOAT TOURS

Almost any boat tour (▶ 19) brings fabulous views of
the Loop's architecture, and the rest of the city strung
along the Lake Michigan shoreline.

THE EL

As they loop the Loop from elevated rails, El trains
on the Brown line bring spectacular close-up views of
the district's high-rise architecture, its streets, and its
parking lots, from unexpected angles.
➕ G/H6/7

*The view from John
Hancock Center's
Skydeck Observatory*

JOHN HANCOCK CENTER
SKYDECK OBSERVATORY

Many Chicagoans prefer this
94th-floor outlook (over
1,000 feet high, and close to
other buildings and the lake)
to the slightly higher but
much busier Sears Tower
Skydeck (▶ 30).
➕ H4 ✉ 875 N. Michigan Avenue
☎ 888/875–VIEW 🕐 Daily
9AM–midnight 🚇 Red line: Chicago
🚌 145, 146, 147, 151 ♿ Good
💰 Moderate

MICHIGAN AVENUE
BRIDGE

Nighttime on this Chicago
River crossing point reveals

Sunrise and the
Lakefront Trail

Early birds can enjoy one of the
best sunrises anywhere in the
Midwest by joining the walkers,
joggers, and bicyclists who start
each morning on the 10-mile
Lakefront Trail through Lincoln
Park (▶ 29). The spectacle
created as the sun comes up
over the lake, its rays reflected
in the buildings of the Loop,
makes the effort to be there
well worth while.

the Wrigley Building and Tribune Tower illuminated
by floodlights; in the other direction loom the
variously lit high-rises of the Loop.
➕ H5/6 ✉ Michigan Avenue between E. Wacker Drive and E. Illinois
Street

LAKE SHORE DRIVE

By car, the best views of Chicago's high-rise skyline
are from Lake Shore Drive, which cuts between the
city and Lake Michigan. Passengers always relish the
spectacle, although on weekdays drivers might well
be too preoccupied with negotiating Chicago's traffic
to enjoy the fine view.

PROMONTORY POINT

From this lakeside outlook some 5 miles south of the
Loop, the Chicago skyline rises in great splendor. To
the east, the curving Lake Michigan shoreline marks
the northern edge of Indiana.
➕ Off map to south ✉ Eastern end of 55th Street

FOR KIDS

ARTIFACT CENTER AT THE SPERTUS MUSEUM

Interactive exhibits guide inquisitive minds through the mysteries of Middle Eastern archeology, and a re-created dig allows young hands to "discover" buried items from early Jewish civilizations, described in wall charts, maps, and explanatory texts.

➕ H7 ✉ 618 S. Michigan Avenue ☎ 312/322–1754 ⏰ Sun–Thu 1–4:30 🚇 Red line: Harrison 🚌 1, 3, 4, 6, 38, 146 ♿ Good 💵 Inexpensive

CHICAGO ACADEMY OF SCIENCES—
THE PEGGY NOTEBAERT NATURE MUSEUM

Lively exhibits explore the natural history of the Midwest, including a 28-foot high greenhouse holding Butterfly Haven, and the inside story on the insect population of every household.

➕ G1 ✉ On the banks of North Pond in Lincoln Park (near Fullerton Parkway) ☎ 773/755–5100 ⏰ Mon–Sun 10–5; Wed 10–8 🚇 Brown and Red lines: Fullerton 🚌 22, 36, 72, 156 ♿ Good 💵 Inexpensive; free Tue

CHICAGO CHILDREN'S MUSEUM

Spread across three floors are scores of lively and entertaining things to do for those aged under 12. These include workshop areas such as the Inventing Lab, where kids can assemble flying machines, and Artabounds where they can create their own murals and sculptures. Programs change daily.

➕ J5 ✉ Navy Pier, 700 E. Grand Avenue ☎ 312/527–1000 ⏰ Tue–Sun 10–5; Thu 10–4, 5–8 🚇 Red line: Grand 🚌 29, 56, 65, 66 ♿ Good 💵 Moderate; free Thu 5–8

LINCOLN PARK ZOO

Lions, cheetahs, gorillas, and chimpanzees are especially popular, along with the Children's Zoo, where tame and usually very furry animals can be stroked and cuddled.

➕ G2 ✉ Lincoln Park ☎ 312/742–2000 ⏰ Daily 9–5; Memorial Day–Labor Day 9–7 🚇 Brown line: Armitage, Fullerton; Red line: Fullerton 🚌 151, 156 ♿ Few 💵 Free

DisneyQuest

Filling five stories and 90,000sq feet, DisneyQuest is the Disney company's indoor theme park with multimedia interactive games, high-tech virtual-reality rides, low-tech arcade games and pinball, and lots more to thrill kids of all ages.

✉ 55 E. Ohio Street
☎ 312/222–1300
⏰ Mon–Wed 11–10; Thu, Fri 11–midnight; Sat 10–midnight; Sun 10–10

Fun and games at the Chicago Children's Museum

WHAT'S FREE

Watching the money-go-round

Speculating on pork belly futures is just one specialty of Chicago's financial dealers. At the Chicago Board of Trade (➤ 31) and the Mercantile Exchange (✉ 30 S. Wacker Drive) visitors who love the sight of money changing hands but do not want to risk a cent watch from public galleries as millions of dollars are made and lost.

HAROLD WASHINGTON LIBRARY CENTER

The U.S.'s largest public library is a state-of-the-art facility. Note its free exhibitions and eye-catching artworks. There is a children's library too.

➕ H7 ✉ 400 S. State Street ☎ 312/747–4300 🕐 Mon 9–7; Tue and Thu 11–7; Wed, Fri–Sat 9–5; Sun 1–5 🚇 Blue line: La Salle 🚌 11, 145, 146, 147 ♿ Good

LOOP SCULPTURES (➤ 16)

Impressive sculptures stand on many plazas of the Loop. Most noteworthy are by Alexander Calder ✉ Federal Center, Dearborn Street; Joan Miró ✉ Washington Street; Marc Chagall ✉ First National Plaza, Dearborn Street; Jean Dubuffet ✉ James R. Thompson Center

Alexander Calder's Flamingo *at the Loop*

MEXICAN FINE ARTS CENTER MUSEUM

Displaying selections from a permanent collection of some 1,200 works by artists of Mexican nationality or descent, this museum also mounts strong and varied temporary exhibitions.

➕ D9 ✉ 1852 W. 19th Street ☎ 312/738–1503 🕐 Tue–Sun 10–5 🚇 Blue line: 18th Street 🚌 18 ♿ Good

NAVY PIER

The rejuvenation of the 1916 Navy Pier was one of the success stories of 1990s Chicago. The scene of all-year festivities, including the Chicago Festival in August, this once neglected area has been transformed into several floors of restaurants, snack stands, specialty shops, and assorted entertainment that are filled by families on weekends. At the eastern edge, the collections of the Smith Museum of Stained Glass Windows add an extra dimension.

➕ J/K5 ✉ 600 E. Grand Avenue ☎ 312/595–PIER 🕐 Businesses have individual hours 🚇 Red line: Grand 🚌 29, 56, 65, 66 ♿ Good

CHICAGO's
where to...

EAT

SHOP

BE ENTERTAINED

STAY

CONTEMPORARY AMERICAN

Prices

Expect to pay per person for a meal, excluding drinks:

$ = Up to $15

$$ = $15–$30

$$$ = $30–$50

$$$$ = Above $50

All the restaurants listed are open daily for lunch and dinner unless otherwise stated.

At the luxury restaurants on these pages, the cost of dinner will easily exceed $70 excluding wine for two people, and lunch will typically cost around $50. Except in these luxury restaurants, dining in Chicago is often less expensive than in other major American cities. Expect to spend $6–$9 per person for breakfast, $8–$14 for lunch, and $15–$25 for dinner excluding drinks and tip.

AMBRIA ($$$$)

A seasonally varied menu mates cuisines of France and the world with impeccable service and an immaculate setting.

➕ G2 ✉ 2300 N. Lincoln Park West ☎ 773/472–5959 🕐 Dinner only. Closed Sun 🚇 Brown line: Sedgwick 🚌 156

CAFÉ ABSINTHE ($$)

Dark, atmospheric, and swanky, and excellent eclectic American cuisine with surprisingly little attitude.

➕ C3 ✉ 1954 W. North Avenue ☎ 773/278–4488 🕐 Dinner only 🚇 Blue line: Damen 🚌 50, 56, 73

CHARLIE TROTTER'S ($$$)

A fashionable dining place with superbly inventive, sometimes eccentric cooking.

➕ F2 ✉ 816 W. Armitage Ave ☎ 773/248–6228 🕐 Dinner only. Closed Sun, Mon 🚇 Brown line: Armitage 🚌 8, 73

FAHRENHEIT ($$–$$$)

A cool blue interior marks one of the city's hottest dining spots. If you can't get a table, soak up the glitzy vibe at the bar.

➕ E4 ✉ 696 N. Milwaukee Avenue ☎ 312/733–7400 🕐 Dinner only. Closed Mon 🚇 Blue line: Chicago 🚌 56, 66

MK ($$–$$$)

The lower case title suggests the understated chic of this former paint factory, which chef Michael Kornick has turned into a venue for trendsetting concoctions, including lobster in many guises.

➕ G5 ✉ 868 N. Franklin Street ☎ 312/482–9179 🚇 Brown line: Chicago 🚌 66

PRINTER'S ROW ($$$)

American regional fare reaches new heights of invention. Game and seafood are specialties.

➕ G7 ✉ 550 S. Dearborn Street ☎ 312/461–0780 🕐 Dinner only Sat. Closed Sun 🚇 Red line: Harrison 🚌 24, 36

SPAGO ($$$$)

This spin-off of the famous Los Angeles restaurant has become a premier dining destination. The food, from chef François Kwaku-Dongo, is exotically accented international.

➕ G5 ✉ 520 N. Dearborn Street ☎ 312/527–3700 🕐 Dinner only Sun 🚇 Red line: Grand Avenue 🚌 22, 36, 65

TOPOLOBAMBO ($$–$$$)

Chef Rick Bayless's bold, imaginative Mexican fare is as good as ever.

➕ G5 ✉ 445 N. Clark Street ☎ 312/661–1434 🕐 Dinner only Fri. Closed Sun–Mon 🚇 Blue line: Clark, Lake 🚌 22

TRIO ($$$$)

Chef Shawn McLain provides startling presentations and flavors. One of the most coveted reservations in town.

➕ Off map to north ✉ 1625 Hinman Avenue, Evanston ☎ 847/733–8746 🕐 Dinner only Sat–Thu. Closed Sun 🚇 Purple line: Davis Street

STEAKS, RIBS & CHOPS

CHICAGO CHOP HOUSE ($$–$$$)

The ribs, steaks, and chops here are large and juicy enough to satisfy even the most demanding red-meat eaters. All meals begin with a fresh green salad and a loaf of wholewheat bread.

✚ G5 ✉ 60 W. Ontario Street ☎ 312/787–7100 🕐 Dinner only weekends 🚇 Red line: Grand 🚌 125

ELI'S THE PLACE FOR STEAK ($$–$$$)

Noted for perfectly cooked T-bone steaks. The liver-and-onion appetizer is worth tasting, and don't miss the cheesecake.

✚ H5 ✉ 215 E. Chicago Avenue ☎ 312/642–1393 🕐 Dinner only weekends 🚇 Red line: Chicago 🚌 3, 66

GENE & GEORGETTI ($$$)

Many feel that this steakhouse—complete with the men's-club decor, gruff waiters, and deliciously thick cuts of meat—is the best in the city. Non-carnivores beware—there's scant choice for you.

✚ G5 ✉ 500 N. Franklin Street ☎ 312/527–3718 🚇 Brown, Purple lines: Merchandise Mart 🚌 20

LAWRY'S THE PRIME RIB ($$–$$$)

The primest of prime rib—the only option on the dinner menu here—is accompanied by such traditional favorites as Yorkshire pudding, mashed potatoes, and salad or an enormous baked potato.

✚ H5 ✉ 100 E. Ontario Street ☎ 312/787–5000 🕐 Dinner only weekends 🚇 Red line: Grand 🚌 125

MORTON'S OF CHICAGO ($$–$$$)

Chicago takes steak seriously, and this is one of the best places to eat it. Porterhouses grilled to perfection are the stock-in-trade.

✚ H4 ✉ 1050 N. State Street ☎ 312/266–4820 🕐 Dinner only 🚇 Red line: Chicago 🚌 36

ROBINSON'S NO. 1 RIBS ($–$$)

A favorite for fall-off-the-bone barbecued ribs, chicken, beef, and pork, served with coleslaw and beans, and a choice of a Robinson's secret sauces made of 17 herbs and spices. At other locations throughout the city.

✚ F2 ✉ 655 W. Armitage Avenue ☎ 312/337–1399 🕐 Dinner only weekends 🚇 Brown line: Armitage 🚌 73

RUTH'S CHRIS STEAKHOUSE ($$–$$$)

The Chicago branch of the big U.S. steakhouse chain opened in 1992 and quickly made its mark. It serves substantial steaks, lamb, veal, and pork, all topped with sizzling butter.

✚ G6 ✉ 431 N. Dearborn Street ☎ 312/321–2725 🕐 Dinner only Sat. Closed Sun 🚇 Blue, Red lines: Jackson 🚌 22, 36

All-nighters

Do you get the munchies at 4AM? You won't go hungry in Chicago. In addition to the Melrose and Tempo (➤ 69), 24-hour options include Hollywood Grill (✉ 1601 W. North Avenue ☎ 773/ 395–1818); 3rd Coast (✉ 1260 N. Dearborn Street ☎ 312/649–0730); and Rock'n'Roll McDonald's (✉ 600 N. Clark Street ☎ 312/664–7940), decked out with hundreds of pieces of rock memorabilia.

FRENCH & ITALIAN

Mexican fare

There's no need to run for the border for Mexican fare and margaritas. Chicago's array of fresh Mex includes Su Casa (✉ 49 E. Ontario Street ☎ 312/943–4041); Chipotle Mexican Grill (✉ 3181 N. Broadway Avenue ☎ 773/525–5250); Maiz (✉ 1942 W. Division Street ☎ 773/862–1801); and Lincoln Park's Twisted Lizard (✉ 1964 N. Sheffield Avenue ☎ 773/929–1414).

FRENCH

CHEZ JOEL ($$$)

Unexpected but welcome in Chicago's Little Italy, this tiny French gem serves delightful bistro dishes like seared duck, steak frites, and braised lamb shank. Request a table in the outdoor garden when weather permits.
✚ E8　✉ 1119 W. Taylor Street ☎ 312/226–6479　🕙 Lunch Mon–Fri; dinner Mon–Sat 🚇 Blue line: Racine 🚌 8

EVEREST ($$$$)

This 40th-floor restaurant commanding spectacular views, beloved of financial wheeler-dealers, offers an updated and sometimes inspiring look at chef Jean Joho's native Alsace. The Loop location, prices, and standards of cooking are all breathtakingly high.
✚ G7　✉ 440 S. La Salle Street ☎ 312/663–8920 🕙 Dinner only. Closed Sun, Mon 🚇 Blue line: La Salle 🚌 22

LA PETITE FOLIE ($$$)

Classical French fare in a minimalist setting in a Hyde Park shopping center. The chef hits a home run with the escargot and smooth crème brulee.
✚ Off map to south　✉ 1504 E. 55th Street ☎ 773/493–1394　🕙 Lunch Tue–Fri; dinner Tue–Sun 🚇 Red line: Garfield 🚌 55th, 56th, 57th 🚌 6, 10

LE FRANÇAIS ($$$$)

Since the 1970s, the impeccable fare and extraordinary wine list have been drawing diners to this classic culinary destination about an hour outside the city.
✚ Off map　✉ 269 S. Milwaukee Avenue, Wheeling ☎ 847/541–7470 🕙 Dinner only Sat–Mon. Closed Sun ❓ Best reached by car

THE DINING ROOM ($$$$)

Spread across two sumptuously furnished floors, this restaurant in the luxurious Ritz-Carlton Hotel offers matchless contemporary French cuisine from the *carte* or as a fixed-price meal.
✚ H5　✉ Ritz-Carlton Hotel, 160 E. Pearson Street ☎ 312/573–5223 🕙 Dinner only 🚇 Red line: Chicago 🚌 125, 157

ITALIAN

BACINO'S STUFFED PIZZA ($–$$)

This is the Loop branch of a city-wide chain; the house specialty is a tasty spinach pizza with a choice of cheeses.
✚ H6　✉ 75 E. Wacker Drive ☎ 312/263–0070 🚇 Brown, Orange lines: State 🚌 16, 44

BRICKS ($–$$)

Innovative pies at this Lincoln Park pizzeria have names like "Ditka" and "The Faithful." The beer selection includes Belgian ales and microbrews.
✚ E1　✉ 1909 N. Lincoln Avenue ☎ 312/255–0851 🕙 Dinner only 🚇 Brown line: Armitage 🚌 11

CLUB LUCKY ($–$$)

The Italian menu is long at this popular venue in trendy and increasingly upscale Bucktown, though the food tends to take second place to the socializing.

✚ H4 ⊠ 1824 W. Wabansia Street ☎ 773/227–2300 Ⓜ Blue line: Damon 🚌 72

COCO PAZZO ($$–$$$)

Delectable, mostly Tuscan cuisine in a comfortable setting enhanced by exposed ceiling beams. Tremendous daily specials and desserts; you can watch as your food is being prepared in the kitchen.

✚ G5 ⊠ 300 W. Hubbard Street ☎ 312/836–0900 Ⓓ Dinner only weekends Ⓜ Red line: Grand 🚌 11, 156

EDWARDO'S NATURAL PIZZA ($–$$)

One of several Chicago branches of a fast-growing chain that serves healthy, nutritious pizzas seasoned with home-grown basil.

✚ G4 ⊠ 1212 N. Dearborn Street ☎ 312/337–4490 Ⓜ Red line: Clark/Division 🚌 11, 70

LA STRADA ($$)

Well-presented, mostly northern Italian fare, served beneath crystal chandeliers in a very elegant setting.

✚ H6 ⊠ 155 N. Michigan Avenue ☎ 312/565–2200 Ⓜ Brown, Orange lines: Randolph 🚌 38, 56, 156

MIA FRANCESCA ($$)

There is always a wait at this favorite of Chicago natives. Excellent seafood specials and wonderful red-sauced fare.

✚ Off map to north ⊠ 3311 N. Clark Street ☎ 773/281–3310 Ⓓ Dinner only Ⓜ Brown, Red, Purple lines: Belmont 🚌 22

SCOOZI! ($$)

A vivacious spot for inventive Italian fare, Scoozi! is huge and often crowded with a young group. Look out for the giant tomato over the door.

✚ G5 ⊠ 410 W. Huron Street ☎ 312/943–5900 Ⓓ Dinner only Sun Ⓜ Brown line: Chicago 🚌 37, 41

SPIAGGIA ($$$)

Steamed mussels in garlic and tomato broth is just one of the specialties of this celebrity favorite. The adjoining Spiaggia Café is less costly and less formal, and serves excellent pizza and pasta dishes.

✚ H4 ⊠ 980 N. Michigan Avenue ☎ 312/280–2750 Ⓓ Dinner only Sun Ⓜ Red line: Chicago 🚌 145, 146, 147, 151

VINCI ($$)

Fashionable decor and rustic cuisine put Vinci on top of the list for many Chicagoans. It can be noisy, but the staff are attentive.

✚ F3 ⊠ 1732 N. Halsted Street ☎ 312/266–1199 Ⓓ Dinner Tue–Sun; brunch Sun. Closed Mon Ⓜ Red line: North Avenue, Clybourn 🚌 20, 72

Chicago pizza

The first deep-dish pizza was created in 1943 at Chicago's Pizzeria Uno. The thick but light crust and a generous smothering of tomato sauce and mozzarella cheese, combined with a variety of toppings, helped make the Chicago pizza a full meal in itself, unlike the thin-crusted New York version. Pizzeria Uno is deservedly as popular as ever.

✚ H5 ⊠ 29 E. Ohio Street ☎ 312/321–1000 Ⓜ Red line: Grand 🚌 36

The finest traditional deep-dish pizza is on the menu also at Gino's East (⊠ 633 N. Wells Street ☎ 312/943–1124 Ⓜ Red line: Chicago 🚌 3, 11, 125, 145, 146, 147, 151) and Lou Malnati's Pizzeria (✚ G5 ⊠ 439 N. Wells Street ☎ 312/828–9800 Ⓜ Brown line: Merchandise Mart 🚌 37, 65, 156).

ASIAN

Dim sum

Served by many Chinese restaurants at lunchtime, dim sum is the term for small dishes wheeled around on trolleys. Stop a server who has dishes that look appetizing and take your pick. Popular dishes include *cha sil bow*—steamed pork bun; *gai bow*—steamed chicken bun; *chern goon*—spring rolls; and *sil mi*—steamed pork and shrimp dumpling. When you've eaten your fill, you will be charged by the plate.

ARUN'S ($$$$)
Superb Thai fare, with subtle spicing reflecting the exceptional talent in the kitchen.
🚼 Off map to north ✉ 4156 N. Kedzie Avenue ☎ 773/539–1909 🕐 Dinner only. Closed Mon 🚇 Brown line: Kedzie 🚌 80, 82

BEN PAO ($$)
Inventive and inspired take on Chinese regional dishes, served under subdued lighting and decor. Dim sum on weekends.
🚼 G5 ✉ 52 W. Illinois Street ☎ 312/222–1888 🚇 Red line: Grand 🚌 36

BUKHARA ($)
From the glass-walled kitchen come succulent tandoori dishes and other northwest India specialties; Indian bread is used to eat with. Try the inexpensive weekday lunch buffet.
🚼 H5 ✉ 2 E. Ontario Street ☎ 312/943–0188 🚇 Red line: Grand 🚌 22

EMPEROR'S CHOICE ($$–$$$)
At this small, intimate restaurant portraits of former Chinese emperors hang above diners feasting on some of Chinatown's most creative seafood dishes. For a special occasion order Peking duck a day in advance.
🚼 G10 ✉ 2238 S. Wentworth Avenue ☎ 312/225–8800 🚇 Red line: Cermak/Chinatown 🚌 24

ITTO SUSHI ($$)
Excellent and affordable sushi and sashimi, prepared before your eyes, plus a varied menu of other Japanese fare.
🚼 F1 ✉ 2616 N. Halsted Street ☎ 773/871–1800 🕐 Closed Sun 🚇 Brown line: Diversey 🚌 8

JAIPUR PALACE ($$)
Mellow decor provides a sensuous backdrop for carefully prepared Indian dishes that range from tandoori specials to vegetarian options.
🚼 H5 ✉ 22 E. Hubbard Street ☎ 312/595–0911 🕐 Dinner only weekends 🚇 Red line: Grand 🚌 22, 29, 36

JOY'S NOODLE AND RICE ($)
Great value Thai dishes served without fuss; portions are modest so order plenty. The patio is lovely on sunny days.
🚼 Off map to north ✉ 3257 N. Broadway ☎ 773/327–8330 🚇 Brown, Red lines: Belmont 🚌 36

KLAY OVEN ($$$)
One of Chicago's most acclaimed Indian restaurants. Traditional dishes are expertly prepared and stylishly presented by attentive, friendly staff in a sumptuous setting.
🚼 G5 ✉ 414 N. Orleans Street ☎ 312/527–3999 🕐 Dinner only weekends. Closed Mon 🚇 Brown line: Merchandise Mart 🚌 37, 41

LE COLONIAL ($$$)
This French-Vietnamese hot spot started in New York, then expanded to LA, San Francisco, and Chicago. Rattan furniture and palm trees

set the mood, as does an exotic drink in the sultry upstairs bar.

✚ H4 ✉ 937 N. Rush Street ☎ 312/255–0088 🍴 Closed Sun lunch 🚇 Red line: Chicago 🚌 145, 146, 147, 151

MANDAR INN ($$)

An impressive array of fiery Szechwan dishes stands out amid the fare from the regions of China on the wide-ranging menu in this convivial spot.

✚ G10 ✉ 2249 S. Wentworth Avenue ☎ 312/842–4014 🍴 Closed Mon 🚇 Red line: Cermak/Chinatown 🚌 24

PASTEUR ($$$)

Red snapper and steamed bass are among the specialties at this inviting, romantic Vietnamese restaurant in Edgewater. Named after the Saigon street where the owners had their family home.

✚ Off map to north ✉ 5525 N. Broadway ☎ 773/878–1061 🚇 Red line: Granville 🚌 136

PENNY'S NOODLE SHOP ($)

This Thai-inspired noodle shop draws raves for both traditional dishes and creative interpretations. There is another branch at Diversey Parkway.

✚ Off map to north ✉ 3400 Sheffield Avenue ☎ 773/281–8222 🚇 Brown, Red, Purple lines: Belmont 🚌 7

STANDARD INDIA ($)

The utilitarian decor is not promising, but the Indian food is good. There is a menu, but

many diners opt for the pricewise buffet.

✚ Off map to north ✉ 917 W. Belmont Avenue ☎ 773/929–1123 🚇 Brown, Red lines: Belmont 🚌 77

STAR OF SIAM ($$)

Hustle and bustle describe this no-frills River North Thai outpost, which serves excellent classics like Pad Thai and chicken satay. The large windows and airy atmosphere are a plus.

✚ H5 ✉ 11 E. Illinois Street ☎ 312/670–0100 🚇 Red line: Grand 🚌 29, 36

SZECHWAN EAST ($$–$$$)

Chic and stylish option for zesty Szechwan dishes. The weekday lunch buffet is a good value.

✚ H5 ✉ 340 E. Ohio Street ☎ 312/255–9200 🚇 Red line: Grand 🚌 3, 66, 157

THAI CLASSIC ($–$$)

The inexpensive lunch specials and wonderful Sunday buffet are worth sampling, but the regular menu is no less impressive. Bring your own bottle.

✚ Off map to north ✉ 3332 N. Clark Street ☎ 773/404–2000 🚇 Red line: Addison 🚌 22

THREE HAPPINESS ($–$$)

This is the right spot for a dim sum lunch or for brunch on Sunday, although it fills up very quickly.

✚ G10 ✉ 209 W. Cermak Road ☎ 312/842–1964 🚇 Red line: Cermak/Chinatown 🚌 24

If you're vegetarian

Most Chinese, Thai, and Vietnamese restaurants offer meat-free versions of their staples, as do Indian eateries; Italian restaurants (▶ 64–65) are another likely possibility. Even amid the chop houses and barbecued rib joints, there's usually some selection. Among the few exclusively vegetarian restaurants try Chicago Diner (✉ 3411 N. Halsted Street ☎ 773/935–6696) and Rose Angelis (✉ 1314 W. Wrightwood Avenue).

GERMAN & EAST EUROPEAN

The taste of Chicago

Chicagoans love to eat and do so with gusto by the thousand at the Taste of Chicago festival, one of the city's most eagerly awaited events, which is held annually in Grant Park. For the 11 days before July 4 around 100 local restaurants dispense their creations at affordable prices from open-front stalls. Free musical entertainment keeps toes tapping.

BERGHOFF RESTAURANT ($–$$)

German staples such as *sauerbraten* and *bratwurst* are served in a cavernous oak-panelled dining room, along with home-brewed German-style beer. Well-prepared American dishes are also on the menu. An institution founded in 1893.
✚ H7 ✉ 17 W. Adams Street ☎ 312/427–3170 ◎ Closed Sun 🚇 Blue, Red lines: Jackson 🚌 1, 7, 60, 126, 151

CHICAGO BRAUHAUS ($$)

German classics like *schnitzel* are served at this Lincoln Square eaterie resembling a Munich beer hall.
✚ Off map to north ✉ 4732 N. Lincoln Avenue ☎ 773/784–4444 ◎ Closed Tue 🚇 Brown line: Western

KRYSTYNA'S CAFE ($)

East European touches distinquish a menu of sandwiches, pizza, and assorted snacks. A handy stop in the Loop for a snack or lunch.
✚ H4 ✉ 8 E. Jackson Boulevard ☎ 312/922–9225 🚇 Blue, Red lines: Jackson 🚌 1, 7, 60, 126

LUTZ CONTINENTAL CAFÉ & PASTRY SHOP ($)

This continental-style café earns high marks for its salads, hearty stews, open-faced sandwiches, and quiches. Decadent German-Austrian desserts include delicious hazelnut tortes and apple cakes.
✚ Off map to north ✉ 2458 W. Montrose Avenue ☎ 773/478–7785 ◎ Closed Mon 🚇 Brown line: Montrose 🚌 80

MAREVA'S ($$$)

Excellent Polish fare in an elegant setting. Try the stuffed pastries known as *pierogi*: they are the best in town.
✚ D4 ✉ 1250 N. Milwaukee Avenue ☎ 773/227–4000 ◎ Dinner only Mon–Fri. Closed Mon 🚇 Blue line: Division 🚌 56

MIRABELL ($$)

This Albany Park spot serves up *schnitzel*, *spätzle*, and other German grub, with exhaustive beer choices. Outdoor seating in summer is a plus.
✚ Off map to north ✉ 3454 W. Addison Avenue ☎ 773/463–1962 ◎ Closed Sun 🚇 Blue line: Addison 🚌 22, 152

RUSSIAN TEA TIME ($$)

Caviar, roast pheasant, iced vodka, and other Russian gastronomic specialties.
✚ H7 ✉ 77 E. Adams Street ☎ 312/360–0000 ◎ Lunch only Mon 🚇 Brown, Orange lines: Adams 🚌 1, 7, 60, 126, 151

SAK'S UKRAINIAN VILLAGE RESTAURANT ($)

A lively favorite for traditional Ukrainian stuffed cabbage, chicken Kiev, soups, and *blintzes*.
✚ C5 ✉ 2301 W. Chicago Avenue ☎ 773/278–4445 ◎ Closed Mon 🚇 Blue line: Damen 🚌 66

QUICK BITES

ANN SATHER'S ($)
A venerable coffee shop where Swedish fare such as cranberry pancakes tops the list of favorites. ✠ Off map to north ✉ 929 W. Belmont Avenue ☎ 773/348–2378 🕐 Breakfast, lunch, dinner 🚇 Brown, Red lines: Belmont 🚌 77

BIG BOWL CAFÉ ($–$$)
Delectable Asian noodle dishes, and much more, served in very big bowls. ✠ G5 ✉ 6 E. Cedar Street ☎ 312/640–8888 🕐 Dinner only Sun 🚇 Brown line: Chicago 🚌 37, 41

ED DEBEVIC'S SHORT ORDER DELUXE ($–$$)
Great burgers, sandwiches, and milkshakes served to the background sound of 1950s and 1960s music. ✠ G5 ✉ 640 N. Wells Street ☎ 312/664–1707 🕐 Breakfast, lunch, dinner 🚇 Brown line: Chicago 🚌 37, 41

LAKEFRONT RESTAURANT ($)
A lively spot with wonderful soups, sandwiches, and other hearty fare. ✠ Off map to north ✉ 3042 N. Broadway ☎ 773/472–9040 🕐 Breakfast, lunch, dinner 🚇 Brown line: Diversey 🚌 36

LOU MITCHELL'S ($)
A friendly modestly sized diner, founded in the 1930s and still serving great omelettes. ✠ F7 ✉ 565 W. Jackson Boulevard ☎ 312/939–3111 🕐 Lunch only. Closed Sun 🚇 Blue line: Clinton 🚌 7, 126

THE MELROSE ($)
A coffee shop whose clientele ranges from breakfasting construction workers to snacking nightclubbers. Enormous menu. ✠ Off map to north ✉ 3233 N. Broadway ☎ 773/327–2060 🕐 Breakfast, lunch, dinner 🚇 Brown, Red lines: Belmont 🚌 36

SOUL KITCHEN ($)
A casual favorite for soul food and New Orleans-inspired dishes. ✠ C3 ✉ 1576 N. Milwaukee Avenue ☎ 773/342–9742 🕐 Dinner only 🚇 Blue line: Damen 🚌 27, 56, 60

TEMPO ($)
Coffee shop with fluffy omelettes served in skillets, sandwiches, steaks, and stir-fry dishes in an otherwise pricey neighborhood. ✠ H4 ✉ 6 E. Chestnut Street ☎ 312/943–4373 🕐 Open 24 hours 🚇 Red line: Chicago 🚌 36

TWIN ANCHORS ($–$$)
Simply the best place for ribs. Once an Al Capone hangout. Go early. ✠ G3 ✉ 1655 N. Sedgwick Street ☎ 312/266–1616 🕐 Dinner only Mon–Fri 🚇 Red line: Clybourn; Brown line: Sedgwick 🚌 37

WISHBONE ($)
A down-home joint with soul food and Cajun specialties. One of several branches. ✠ F6 ✉ 1001 W. Washington Street ☎ 312/850–2663 🕐 Closed Sun–Mon 🚌 20

Chicago hot dogs
To a Chicagoan, a hot dog is not merely a frank in a bun. The true Chicago hot dog is a Viennese beef sausage smeared with ketchup, mustard, relish, onions, and hot peppers to taste. Brightly lit hot-dog outlets are a feature of the city, and each has its devotees. If you love great food, sample Gold Coast Dogs—heaven. ✠ H5 ✉ 418 N. State Street, and other locations throughout the city ☎ 312/527–1222 🕐 Breakfast, lunch, dinner. Closed Sat–Sun 🚇 Red line: Grand 🚌 29, 36

MALLS & DEPARTMENT STORES

Chinatown shopping

For shoppers who venture from the better-known retail areas into Chinatown (➤ 50), rewards are plentiful in the form of entertaining emporia squeezed between the countless restaurants that line Wentworth Avenue immediately south of Cermak Road. Check out World Treasures, stocked with Asian delights, and Woks 'n' Things, selling kitchen utensils and general gifts. Within a few strides, you can also pick up a bag of fortune cookies at Fortella and have your face or palm read at Nature Field.

THE ATRIUM MALL

Diverse stores provide an excellent excuse to stroll around the spectacular second floor of this dazzling atrium, a pastiche of glass, marble, and steel, with an impressive waterfall.

H6 ✉ James R. Thompson Center, 100 W. Randolph Street ☎ 312/346–0777 Ⓜ Blue, Brown, Orange lines: Clark/Lake 🚌 156

CARSON PIRIE SCOTT & CO. STORE

Though better known for its exterior architecture (➤ 34), the store has provided middle-class Chicagoans with good clothing, cosmetics, and household accessories for years.

H6 ✉ 1 S. State Street ☎ 312/641–7000 Ⓜ Blue line: Madison; Red line: Monroe 🚌 22, 23, 36, 56, 157

CENTURY SHOPPING CENTER

Many visit this former theater to use its gym on the top floor, so you can watch the buff and tanned parade up the Guggenheimesque circular stairs while you shop at the center's well-known chain stores, mostly clothing specialists, and intriguing locally based specialty shops.

F1 ✉ 2828 N. Clark Street ☎ 773/929–8100 Ⓜ Brown line: Diversey 🚌 22, 36, 76

CHICAGO PLACE

A seven-floor branch of Saks Fifth Avenue department store is an anchor tenant among the classy retailers in this towering construction. Drop into Chiasso to admire artworks and ornaments, explore the Slavic gifts and art in Russian Creations, or snap up an affordable city souvenir in Hello Chicago. There is a food hall on the top floor.

H4 ✉ 700 N. Michigan Avenue ☎ 312/266–7710 Ⓜ Red line: Chicago 🚌 145, 146, 147, 151

THE JEWELER'S CENTER

Jewelry and related products are sold in more than 140 outlets on 13 floors; if you can't find what you're looking for here, you never will.

H6 ✉ 5 S. Wabash Avenue ☎ 312/853–2057 Ⓜ Brown, Orange lines: Madison 🚌 38

MARSHALL FIELD'S

Chicagoans adore this department store, which carries clothing, household goods, jewelry, exotic foods, books, and more. There are several branches in Chicago, but this is the best. The building has a Tiffany-glass dome, and the interior design outdoes Carson Pirie Scott and adds glamor. The store's own Frango Mints, sold in the basement Market Place section, make a good Chicagoland souvenir.

H6 ✉ 111 N. State Street ☎ 312/781–1000 Ⓜ Blue, Red lines: Washington 🚌 6, 11, 29, 36, 44, 62, 146

NAVY PIER

Some 60 stores are gathered in this complex of restaurants and entertainments. If you're ready to buy souvenirs as gifts, this is not a bad place to trawl.

➕ J5 ✉ 700 E. Grand Avenue ☎ 312/595–PIER ⓠ Red line: Grand 🚌 29, 56, 65, 66

NEIMAN-MARCUS

Exclusive, elegant clothing is the forte of handsome Neiman-Marcus, which also sells beauty products and fancy food stuffs. Looking around is good fun, even if you can't afford to buy.

➕ H5 ✉ 737 N. Michigan Avenue ☎ 312/642–5900 ⓠ Red line: Chicago 🚌 145, 146, 147, 151

900 NORTH MICHIGAN

This gleaming marble high-rise consumes an entire city block. Restaurants, movie theaters, and stores are grouped around a six-story atrium; a branch of New York's Bloomingdale's is an anchor. There are also many smaller, exclusive stores, including Gucci and Gallery Lara, where exquisite glass sculptures sell for tens of thousands of dollars.

➕ H4 ✉ 900 N. Michigan Avenue ☎ 312/915–3900 ⓠ Red line: Chicago 🚌 145, 146, 147, 151

SHOPS AT THE MART

Most of the vast Merchandise Mart is closed to the public, except for the first two floors, which woo shoppers with clothing stores, gift shops, and the ubiquitous food court. For more than 50 years, the Kennedy dynasty owned this River North behemoth.

➕ G5 ✉ 350 N. Wells Street ⓠ Brown, Purple lines: Merchandise Mart 🚌 37

WATER TOWER PLACE

Packing these seven floors are clothing stores for men, women, and children that span Abercrombie & Fifth, North Beach Leather, Baby Gap, and Victoria's Secret. There are also jewelers, art galleries, home-furnishing emporiums such as Brookstone and Chiasso, and perfumeries. In addition, there are movie theaters and restaurants, and specialty retailers such as Accent Chicago and the Water Tower Check Shop. You can rest next to the indoor shrubbery and waterfalls, or be decadent and treat yourself to some Godiva chocolates.

➕ H4 ✉ 835 N. Michigan Avenue ☎ 312/440–3165 ⓠ Red line: Chicago 🚌 145, 146, 147, 151

ZEMSKY'S

Don't come here looking for posh designer labels, but expect reasonably priced clothing for men, women, and children. Home furnishings are also part of the inventory. There are five locations throughout Chicago.

➕ B10 ✉ 2740 W. Cermak Road ☎ 773/247–4600 ⓠ Blue: California

The making of the Magnificent Mile

No Chicago shopper could be unaware that most high-end stores are gathered along the section of Michigan Avenue known as the Magnificent Mile (➤ 51). Many stores appeared here following the 1920s opening of the river bridge linking Michigan Avenue to the Loop, but the "Magnificent Mile" concept was a 1940s idea that eventually mutated into today's rows of marble-clad towers, mostly built during the 1970s and 1980s.

CLOTHES

Curious clothing

Should the sensible buying of sensible clothes for sensible everyday wear suddenly become a stultifyingly dull pursuit, you can let your sartorial imaginations run riot at Chicago Costume Company (✉ 1120 W. Fullerton Parkway). This enormous store carries hundreds of outrageous costumes, masks, and assorted outlandish accessories, for sale or rent, for the dresser who dares.

AGNES B

When money is no object look to this chic French designer to help you look like a sophisticated Parisian woman. Just off Michigan Avenue.
✚ H5 ✉ 46 E. Walton Street ☎ 312/642–7483 🚇 Red line: Chicago 🚌 145, 146, 147, 151

BANANA REPUBLIC

The hugely popular local branch of the nationally known supplier of quality casualwear.
✚ H5 ✉ 744 N. Michigan Avenue ☎ 312/642–0020 🚇 Red line: Chicago 🚌 145, 146, 147, 151

BARNEYS NEW YORK

The Chicago branch of a Manhattan store noted for chic women's clothing and its fine menswear.
✚ H4 ✉ 25 E. Oak Street ☎ 312/587–1700 🚇 Red line: Chicago 🚌 145, 146, 147, 151

BROOKS BROTHERS

Well-made attire for men, in conservative styles, plus some equally straight forward clothing for women.
✚ H5 ✉ 713 N. Michigan Avenue ☎ 312/915–0060 🚇 Red line: Chicago 🚌 145, 146, 147, 151

CHANEL BOUTIQUE

Breath in the expensive perfumes, browse the top-of-the-line women's clothing, and eye the gorgeous baubles in the jewelry section; its all in a day's shopping for the well-dressed and seriously wealthy.
✚ H4 ✉ 935 N. Michigan Drive (in the Drake Hotel) ☎ 312/787–5500 🚇 Red line: Chicago 🚌 145, 146, 147, 151

J. CREW

Classic modern clothes, shoes, and accessories for young men and women at work and play.
✚ H4 ✉ 900 N. Michigan Avenue ☎ 312/751–2739 🚇 Red line: Chicago 🚌 145, 146, 147, 151

LORD & TAYLOR

Lovely, classic clothes, shoes, and accessories for men and women in Water Tower Place.
✚ H4 ✉ Water Tower Place, 835 N. Michigan Avenue ☎ 312/787–7400 🚇 Red line: Chicago 🚌 145, 146, 147, 151

PETITE SOPHISTICATE

An impressive assortment of stylish business and leisure clothing for smaller-than-average women.
✚ H4 ✉ 700 N. Michigan Avenue ☎ 312/787–4923 🚇 Red line: Chicago 🚌 145, 146, 147, 151

PRADA

Three-levels of clothing and accessories from the Italian designer.
✚ H4 ✉ 30 E. Oak Street ☎ 312/951–1113 🚇 Red line: Chicago 🚌 145, 146, 147, 151

SULKA

If you have money, this is the place to be fitted out in a quality hand-made suit; if not, ogle the hand-crafted silk ties.
✚ H4 ✉ 55 E. Oak Street ☎ 312/951–9500 🚇 Red line: Chicago 🚌 145, 146, 147, 151

ACCESSORIES & VINTAGE CLOTHES

BEATNIX

Packed from floor to ceiling, this stash of wild and unbelievable attire is Disneyland for the daring dresser.

✚ Off map to north ✉ 3400 N. Halsted Avenue ☎ 773/281–6933 🚇 Brown, Red lines: Belmont 🚌 152

FLASHY TRASH

Chicago's major trove of vintage clothing, ranging from Victorian evening wear to 1970s disco duds.

✚ Off map to north ✉ 3524 N. Halsted Street ☎ 773/327–6900 🚇 Red line: Addison 🚌 152

GREAT LAKES SILVER

Baltic amber features along the large selection of otherwise mostly silver jewelry; look out for the ultra-pricey belt buckles and the designer sunglasses.

✚ H4 ✉ 104 E. Oak Street ☎ 312/266–2211 🚇 Red line: Chicago 🚌 145, 146, 147, 151

HERMÈS OF PARIS

Chicago branch of the Parisian fashion house, and a certainty for lovely scarves, handbags, ties, and leather items.

✚ H4 ✉ 110 E. Oak Street ☎ 312/787–8175 🚇 Red line: Chicago 🚌 145, 146, 147, 151

HOLLYWOOD MIRROR

Two floors packed with colorful garb of recent decades, mostly women's apparel but also menswear, plus a collection of lamps, jewelry, and oddities. The stock has been carefully culled—unlike the clothes at Ragstock, upstairs—so prices are higher.

✚ Off map to north ✉ 812 Belmont Street ☎ 773/404–4510 🚇 Brown, Red lines: Belmont 🚌 77

RAGSTOCK

The quantity of used clothing is huge, and prices are very low. It takes time to sort through the dross, but you can find some great bargains. Upstairs from Hollywood Mirror.

✚ Off map to north ✉ 812 Belmont Street ☎ 773/868–9263 🚇 Brown, Red lines: Belmont 🚌 77

SILVER MOON

Bargains are few but the wares are beautiful in this sizable emporium of vintage clothing. Look for immaculate 1920s evening wear.

✚ Off map to north ✉ 3337 N. Halsted Street ☎ 773/883–0222 🚇 Red line: Addison 🚌 152

TIFFANY & CO.

The famous New York jeweler offers a stunning assortment of stones, plus superb watches, crystal, china, and more.

✚ H4 ✉ 730 N. Michigan Avenue ☎ 312/944–7500 🚇 Red line: Chicago 🚌 145, 146, 147, 151

URBAN OUTFITTERS

The hippest accessories, to match the up-to-the-minute clothes and the funky items for the home.

✚ H4 ✉ 935 E. Walton Street ☎ 312/640–1919 🚇 Red Line: Chicago 🚌 145, 146, 147, 151

Button up!

At Tender Buttons (✉ 946 N. Rush Street) the thousands of buttons in thousands of styles on sale are displayed with a museum-like reverence, and are complemented by a fine selection of Edwardian cufflinks.

ART, ANTIQUES & COLLECTIBLES

Collectibles from far corners

Artworks and other items from the far-flung corners of the globe are the stock-in-trade of two Chicago stores. Arms Akimbo (✉ 233 W. Muron Street) sells tribal and cultural art and antiquities, including masks, textiles, and sculpture from Africa. The Alaska Shop (✉ 104 E. Oak Street) has works created by the Inuit people of Alaska, Canada, and Siberia.

BROADWAY ANTIQUES MARKET

The 85 dealers at this two-story antiques haven sell everything from art deco to mid-20th century modern.
✚ Off map to north ✉ 6130 N. Broadway Avenue ☎ 773/743–5444 🚇 Red line: Granville 🚌 136

CHRISTA'S LTD

Stuffed with predominantly 18th- and 19th-century fare, including tables, bureaux, cabinets, crystalware, mirrors, lamps, clocks, and much more from Europe and the U.S.
✚ G5 ✉ 217 W. Illinois Street ☎ 312/222–2520 🚇 Red line: Grand 🚌 65

FLY BY NITE GALLERY

A clutter of art-deco jewelry and ceramics, and more objets d'art than you can shake a stick at.
✚ G5 ✉ 714 N. Wells Street ☎ 312/664–8136 🚇 Brown line: Chicago 🚌 37, 41

JAY ROBERT'S ANTIQUE WAREHOUSE

You'll find everything from clocks to fireplaces among the antiques and junk that fill 50,000sq feet of floor space here.
✚ G5 ✉ 149 W. Kinzie Street ☎ 312/222–0167 🚇 Brown, Purple lines: Merchandise Mart 🚌 36, 62

POSTER PLUS

Historic posters, mostly celebrating landmarks in Chicago and U.S. history, though many are attractive reprints rather than originals.
✚ H7 ✉ 200 S. Michigan Avenue ☎ 312/461–9277 🚇 Brown, Orange lines: Adams 🚌 3, 4, 6, 38

R. H. LOVE GALLERIES

Housed in a 19th-century mansion, the extensive and expensive selection of American art from all eras is particularly strong on Impressionists.
✚ H5 ✉ 40 E. Erie Street ☎ 312/640–1300 🚇 Red line: Chicago, Grand 🚌 22, 36

SALVAGE ONE

Five floors of warehouse space is chock-full of light fixtures, fireplace mantels, bar stools, tables, and many more architectural artifacts.
✚ F8 ✉ 1524 S. Sangamon Street ☎ 312/733–0098 🚇 Red line: Addison 🚌 8

STEVE STARR STUDIOS

A wonderful selection of original art-deco paraphernalia, ranging from silver cigarette cases to chrome cocktail shakers.
✚ E1 ✉ 2779 N. Lincoln Avenue ☎ 773/525–6530 🚇 Brown line: Diversey 🚌 11, 76

VINTAGE POSTERS INTERNATIONAL

Stylish posters from the U.S. and Europe dating from the 1880s, plus a diverse selection of French decorative items of the belle époque.
✚ G3 ✉ 1551 N. Wells Street ☎ 312/951–6681 🚇 Brown line: Sedgwick 🚌 135, 156

BOOKS

AFTER-WORDS

New titles on most subjects but leaning towards less-than-mainstream fiction, politics, and history; plus a gigantic stock of used books on all subjects.

✚ G5 ✉ 23 E. Illinois Street ☎ 312/464–1110 Ⓜ Red line: Grand 🚌 22, 29, 36

BARBARA'S BOOKSTORE

Old, new, and otherwise hard-to-find literature, plus political and contemporary lifestyle titles. Other branches throughtout the city.

✚ G3 ✉ 1350 N. Wells Street ☎ 312/642–5044 Ⓜ Brown line: Sedgwick; Red line: Clark/Division 🚌 11, 156

CHICAGO ARCHITECTURE FOUNDATION

Exemplary source of books on architecture.

✚ H7 ✉ 224 S. Michigan Avenue ☎ 312/922–3432 Ⓜ Brown, Orange lines: Adams 🚌 3, 4, 6, 38

CHICAGO RARE BOOK CENTER

Intriguing assortment of first editions and other volumes that span fiction, history, the arts, travel, and many more subjects. Also has a browse-worthy stock of historic maps and photos of Chicago in poster form.

✚ G4 ✉ 56 W. Maple Street ☎ 312/988–7246 Ⓜ Red line: Chicago 🚌 22

57TH STREET BOOKS

Hyde Park institution, with both new and used volumes. Toys are provided for children of browsing parents.

✚ Off map to south ✉ 1301 E. 57th Street ☎ 773/684–1300 Ⓜ Red line: Garfield 🚇 55th, 56th, 57th Street 🚌 1, 4, 28, 51

QUIMBY'S BOOKSTORE

Alternative bookstore selling every title imaginable.

✚ D3 ✉ 1854 W. North Avenue ☎ 773/342–0910 Ⓜ Blue line: Damen 🚌 56

RAIN DOG BOOKS

Antique and rare titles.

✚ H7 ✉ 404 S. Michigan Avenue ☎ 312/922–1200 Ⓜ Red line: Harrison 🚌 1, 7, 126

RAND MCNALLY MAP STORE

Atlases, regional and city street maps; guidebooks.

✚ H5 ✉ 444 N. Michigan Avenue ☎ 312/321–1751 Ⓜ Red line: Grand 🚌 3, 11, 145, 146, 147, 151

UNABRIDGED BOOKSTORE

General bookstore with a large children's section, travel, and titles of interest to gays and lesbians.

✚ Off map to north ✉ 3251 N. Broadway ☎ 773/883–9119 Ⓜ Brown, Red lines: Belmont 🚌 136

WOMEN & CHILDREN FIRST

Women's-interest and children's titles; fiction.

✚ Off map to north ✉ 5233 N. Clark Street ☎ 773/769–9299 Ⓜ Red line: Berwyn 🚌 22

Printer's Row bookstores

A cluster of noteworthy bookstores lies just south of the Loop in Printer's Row (➤ 51). Prairie Avenue Bookshop (✉ 418 S. Wabash Avenue) stocks seemingly every tome on architecture and town planning ever published. Sandmeyer's Bookstore (✉ 714 S. Dearborn Street) is strong on travel titles. Powell's Bookstore (✉ 828 S. Wabash Avenue) carries secondhand books on all subjects.

National chains

The Diversey branch of Barnes & Noble (✉ 659 W. Diversey Parkway ☎ 773/871–9004 Ⓜ Brown line: Diversey 🚌 22, 36, 76) is a superstore, with shelf after shelf of general titles, newspapers, and magazines, in an atmosphere conducive to browsing. Borders Books & Music (✉ 830 N. Michigan Avenue ☎ 312/573–0564 Ⓜ Red line: Chicago 🚌 145, 146, 147, 151) has a comparably huge selection. Both have cafés.

SHOPS & OUTLETS

Long-distance discount shopping

Two major outlet malls on the edge of the Chicago area are worth the trip. An hour or so's ride west finds Gurnee Mills (☎ 800/937–7467), whose 200-plus stores are easily combined with a trip to Six Flags Great America (► 21). An hour south in Michigan City, Indiana, is Lighthouse Place (☎ 219/879–6506), another extensive group of factory retail outlets.

CRATE & BARREL OUTLET
A small factory outlet with hefty discounts on the admirable Crate & Barrel housewares, furniture, and home accessories.
🔲 F3 ✉ 800 W. North Avenue ☎ 312/787–4775 🚇 Brown line: Sedgwick

DESIGNER RESALE
Names such as Armani and Chanel are among the designer labels offered secondhand in this chic womenswear boutique.
🔲 G5 ✉ 658 N. Dearborn Street ☎ 312/587–3312 🚇 Red line: Grand 🚌 22

DISGRACELAND
Contemporary used clothes from stores like Urban Outfitters, Contempo, and Banana Republic.
🔲 Off map to north ✉ 3338 N. Clark Street ☎ 773/281–5875 🚇 Red line: Belmont 🚌 22

FILENE'S BASEMENT
Formidably large stock—spread over several floors—of designer clothing and accessories for men and women at 30 to 60 percent off retail prices.
🔲 H4 ✉ 830 N. Michigan Avenue ☎ 312/482–8918 🚇 Red line: Chicago 🚌 145, 146, 147, 151
Also at:
🔲 G6 ✉ 1 N. State Street

FOX'S
Recent and current women's designer clothing—for business, sport, and casual wear—at discounted prices.
🔲 F1 ✉ 2150 N. Halsted ☎ 773/281–0700 🚇 Brown, Red lines: Fullerton 🚌 8

GAP FACTORY OUTLET
Big discounts on Gap and Banana Republic stock.
🔲 B/C2 ✉ 2778 N. Milwaukee Avenue ☎ 773/252–0594 🚇 Blue line: Western

MCSHANE'S EXCHANGE
The latest designer clothing for women, barely worn and temptingly priced.
🔲 F2 ✉ 1141 W. Webster Avenue ☎ 773/525–0211 🚇 Brown line: Armitage 🚌 73

RECYCLE
Row after row of mid-range designer clothing for men and women fills this aircraft-hanger-like space—at very affordable prices.
🔲 C3 ✉ 1474 N. Milwaukee Avenue ☎ 773/645–1900 🚇 Blue line: Damen 🚌 56

THE SECOND CHILD
Designer children's clothes, furnishings, and toys, secondhand but in excellent condition.
🔲 E2 ✉ 954 W. Armitage Avenue ☎ 773/883–0880 🚇 Brown line: Armitage 🚌 73

ULTIMATELY YOURS
Huge stock of mostly women's designer clothing, plus some menswear, at prices to brag about. Also shoes and accessories.
🔲 Off map to north ✉ 2931 N. Broadway Avenue ☎ 773/975–1581 🚇 Brown, Red lines: Belmont 🚌 36

MISCELLANEOUS

AMERICAN GIRL PLACE

A landmark for girls who love the eponymous dolls. Everything here is American Girl—clothes, books, stage shows, lessons in etiquette, afternoon tea, and lots more. For some, a shrine.

✚ G5 ✉ 111 E. Chicago Avenue ☎ 877/AG–PLACE or 312/943–9400 🚇 Red line: Chicago 🚌 11, 66

ARCHITECTURAL REVOLUTION

Garden gnomes, pseudo-Roman columns, and other wacky decorative items.

✚ Off map to north ✉ 3220 N. Clark Street ☎ 773/752–7837 🚇 Brown, Red lines: Belmont

CHICAGO MUSIC MART

Pianos, *ocarina*, and Indian *tablas* are among the instruments you can find at this gathering of music retailers. Or look for the musically themed sweets.

✚ H7 ✉ 333 S. State Street ☎ 312/362–6700 🚇 Blue, Red lines: Jackson 🚌 1, 7, 60, 126, 145, 146, 147, 151

CRATE & BARREL

Stylish and reasonably priced kitchenware, furniture, and household accessories. Also ➤ 76.

✚ H5 ✉ 646 N. Michigan Avenue 🚇 Red line: Chicago 🚌 145, 146, 147, 151

JAZZ RECORD MART

Mainstream releases and cult rarities are among its thousands of CDs,

records, and tapes.

✚ G5 ✉ 444 N. Wabash Avenue ☎ 312/222–1467 🚇 Red line: Grand 🚌 22, 29, 36

NIKE TOWN

Even if you couldn't care less about Nike sportswear, a visit to this pulsating, themed, tri-level store—complete with aquarium—is a must.

✚ H5 ✉ 669 N. Michigan Avenue ☎ 312/642–6363 🚇 Red line: Chicago 🚌 145, 146, 147, 151

THE SAVVY TRAVELLER

Everything travelers might need—from money belts to guidebooks.

✚ H7 ✉ 310 S. Michigan Avenue ☎ 312/913–9800 🚇 Brown, Orange lines: Adams 🚌 3, 4, 6, 38

SONY GALLERY OF CONSUMER ELECTRONICS

Despite the museum-like displays, this really is a store for showcasing Sony's latest items. Slim-screen computers, memory sticks, wide-screen TVs, and Playstations are all here.

✚ H4 ✉ 633 N. Michigan Avenue ☎ 312/943–3334 🚇 Red line: Chicago 🚌 145, 146, 147, 151

TOWER RECORDS

Every record or CD ever released in any musical category (it seems), plus books and videos.

✚ G2 ✉ 2301 N. Clark Street ☎ 773/477–5994 🚇 Brown, Red lines: Fullerton 🚌 22, 36

Cigars and more

Chicago's several stores for discerning smokers offer quality hand-rolled cigars and, usually, imported cigarettes and smokers' accessories. Three of the best are Old Chicago Smoke Shop (✉ 10 S. La Salle Street), Blue Havana (✉ 46 E. Oak Street), and Little Havana (✉ 6 W. Maple Street and at Navy Pier, ➤ 60).

BLUES & JAZZ SPOTS

Grant Park's blues and jazz

Each June and September the Petrillo Music Shell in Grant Park (► 41) is the stage for blues and jazz festivals respectively, which draw top international names as well as the city's greats in both fields. The performers are greeted by tens of thousands of their admirers, who arrive with blankets and picnic supplies to enjoy the free music.

ANDY'S JAZZ CLUB

Popular and unpretentious jazz venue that earns its keep by staging commendable sets on weekday lunchtimes, as well as early and mid-evening shows.

✚ H5 ✉ 11 E. Hubbard Street ☎ 312/642–6805 🚇 Red line: Grand 🚌 29, 36

BE-BOP CAFÉ

Listen to be-bop and other jazz while tucking into jambalaya, barbecued ribs, and other cajun dishes. Popular among music fans and tourists alike.

✚ J/K5 ✉ Navy Pier, 600 E. Grand Avenue ☎ 312/595–5299 🚌 29, 55, 65, 66

BLUE CHICAGO

Comfortable homey blues club, showcasing home-grown musical talent.

✚ G5 ✉ 736 N. Clark Street ☎ 312/642–6261 🚇 Red line: Chicago 🚌 22, 36

B.L.U.E.S.

Small, dimly lit, but very atmospheric spot to hear some of the best blues artists around, including some legendary old-timers.

✚ F1 ✉ 2519 N. Halsted Street ☎ 773/528–1012 🚇 Brown, Red lines: Fullerton 🚌 8

BUDDY GUY'S LEGENDS

Co-owner and famed blues guitarist Buddy Guy presents outstanding blues acts, including internationally known names and local rising stars.

✚ H7 ✉ 754 S. Wabash Avenue ☎ 312/427–0333 🚇 Red line: Harrison 🚌 12

GREEN MILL

The jazz here is always good, sometimes brilliant. On Sunday nights, poets take to the stage for competitive poetry reading—more entertaining than you might think. Well north of downtown in an unfashionable part of the city, but worth the journey.

✚ F1 ✉ 4802 N. Broadway ☎ 773/878–5552 🚇 Brown line: Diversey 🚌 136

HOUSE OF BLUES

Blues and rock from around the city, the country, and the world every night of the week. The smaller Back Porch stage has blues nightly, and is open at lunch for more of the same.

✚ G5 ✉ 329 N. Dearborn Street ☎ 312/923–2000 🚇 Red line: Grand 🚌 22, 36, 62

JAZZ SHOWCASE

Photos of jazz legends decorate this historic joint, and big names in contemporary jazz play here. Bring the kids to the Sunday matinee performances.

✚ G5 ✉ 59 W. Grand Avenue ☎ 312/670–2473 🚇 Red line: Grand 🚌 22, 65

KINGSTON MINES

Likeably medium-sized venue with live nightly blues on two stages.

✚ Off map to north ✉ 2548 N. Halsted Street ☎ 773/477–4646 🚇 Brown, Red lines: Fullerton 🚌 8

COMEDY, FOLK, ROCK & REGGAE SPOTS

BEAT KITCHEN
Smallish venue that makes a good setting for folk and rock acts, predominantly from around Chicago.
✚ Off map to north ✉ 2100 W. Belmont Avenue ☎ 773/281–4444 🚇 Brown, Red lines: Belmont 🚌 22

CUBBY BEAR LOUNGE
Its location opposite Wrigley Field makes this sports bar a favorite spot for post-Cub games. Live music spans rock, country, reggae, and blues. Dancing and beer.
✚ Off map to north ✉ 1059 W. Addison Street ☎ 773/327–1662 🚇 Brown line: Addison 🚌 22, 152

ELBO ROOM
Innovative two-floored venue for live alternative rock, often featuring hot new acts, poetry readings, and comedy.
✚ Off map to north ✉ 2871 N. Lincoln Avenue ☎ 773/549–5549 🚇 Brown line: Diversey 🚌 11

HOT HOUSE
Trendy, warehouse-like spot in South Loop area, with eclectic music and an arty crowd.
✚ H7 ✉ 31 W. Balbo Drive ☎ 312/362–9707 🚇 Red line: Harrison 🚌 6, 146

IMPROVOLYMPIC
House comedians perform improvised sketches and entire musicals based on audience suggestions. Fridays and Saturdays are busiest; earlier crowds are smaller and admission may be free.
✚ Off map to north ✉ 3541 N. Clark Street ☎ 773/880–0199 🚇 Brown, Red lines: Belmont 🚌 22, 156

KITTY O'SHEA'S
Ersatz Irish pub with real Irish music, inside the Chicago Hilton and Towers hotel (▶ 84).
✚ H7 ✉ 720 S. Michigan Avenue ☎ 800/HILTONS or 312/922–4400 🚇 Red line: Harrison 🚌 1, 3, 4, 6, 146

METRO
The city's major mid-sized venue for live rock, with ample space for dancing and plentiful seating with good views. Other levels have a nightclub and coffee bar.
✚ Off map to north ✉ 3730 N. Clark Street ☎ 773/549–0203 🚇 Brown line: Addison 🚌 22, 152

OLD TOWN SCHOOL OF FOLK MUSIC
Dedicated to folk music, with two nightly shows from leading folksters.
✚ E2 ✉ 909 W. Armitage Avenue ☎ 773/525–7793 🚇 Brown line: Armitage 🚌 73

THE WILD HARE & SINGING ARMADILLO FROG SANCTUARY
Top-notch live reggae and other Caribbean and African sounds.
✚ Off map to north ✉ 3530 N. Clark Street ☎ 773/327–4273 🚇 Brown line: Addison 🚌 22, 152

ZANIES
Small, enjoyable comedy club, featuring rising local stars as well as better-known names.
✚ G3 ✉ 1548 N. Wells Street ☎ 312/337–4027 🚇 Brown line: Sedgwick 🚌 11, 156

Can you croon in tune
Karaoke supplies plenty of laughs as long as you have the key ingredient: a lively group that isn't afraid to embarrass itself by singing in public with a machine that serves up the words and music. If you're in the "Windy City" on a Tuesday, head over to Circuit (✉ 3641 N. Halsted ☎ 773/325–2233). Working Man's (✉ 4400 W. Diversey ☎ 773/736–4830) has karaoke on Fridays, and on Thursdays the place is Original Mother's (✉ 26 W. Division Street ☎ 312/642–7251), also familiar as the watering hole patronized by Rob Lowe and Demi Moore in the film *About Last Night*.

CLASSICAL MUSIC, THEATER & THE PERFORMING ARTS

ANNOYANCE THEATER

Searing comedy and spoofs, much of it developed from improvised sketches; audience participation is encouraged.

✚ Off map to north ✉ 3747 N. Clark Street ☎ 773/929–6200 🚇 Red line: Addison 🚌 36

AUDITORIUM THEATER

Designed by the revered Adler & Sullivan partnership, the marvelously renovated Auditorium Building, which holds the theater, was the world's heaviest structure when completed in 1889. Excellent acoustics and good sightlines make it a fine venue for dance, music, and drama productions.

✚ H7 ✉ 50 E. Congress Parkway ☎ 312/922–2110 🚇 Red line: Harrison 🚌 6, 145, 146, 147, 151

CHICAGO THEATER

Broadway blockbusters, local shows, and star-studded musical events grace the stage, though an equal attraction is the building itself—an ornate 1920s movie palace, now restored.

✚ G6 ✉ 175 N. State Street ☎ 312/902–1500 🚇 Red line: Washington 🚌 6, 11, 29, 36, 44, 62, 145, 146

CHICAGO THEATER COMPANY

This African-American company stages some of the city's best contemporary productions at theaters around town.

The repertoire mixes original material with adaptations.

✚ Off map to south ✉ 500 E. 67th Street ☎ 773/493–0901 🚌 3

CIVIC OPERA HOUSE

The fine Lyric Opera of Chicago company performs from mid-September to early February at this art-deco auditorium (which is also one of the main dance venues). Seats are sometimes available at the box office on the day of performance.

✚ G6 ✉ 20 N. Wacker Drive ☎ 312/419–0033 🚇 Brown, Orange lines: Madison/Wells 🚌 129

DANCE CENTER OF COLUMBIA COLLEGE

The 272-seat theater makes an intimate setting for productions by the Columbia dance college students; some feature internationally known artists.

✚ H8 ✉ 1306 S. Michigan Avenue ☎ 312/344–8300 🚇 Brown, Orange, Red lines: Roosevelt 🚌 1, 3, 4

FORD CENTER FOR THE PERFORMING ARTS/ORIENTAL THEATER

Still called the Oriental by locals, this ornate, 2,180-seat theater reopened in 1998 after a painstaking restoration. The North Loop theater presents first-rate shows in its top-notch performance space.

✚ H6 ✉ 24 W. Randolph Street ☎ 312/782–2004 🚇 Red, Brown, Green, Orange lines: Lake 🚌 156

Ravinia Festival

From mid-June to Labor Day, the northern suburb of Highland Park plays host to the Ravinia Festival. The summer home of the Chicago Symphony Orchestra, Ravinia also stages rock and jazz concerts, dance events, and other cultural activities. Chartered buses ferry festival-goers the 25 miles from central Chicago; you can also get there by commuter train. For further details ☎ 800/433–8819

GOODMAN THEATER

Adjoining the Art Institute of Chicago (▶ 40), the Goodman hosts some of the best drama in the city, including both classics and cutting-edge contemporary productions. The latter are often staged in the smaller of the building's two auditoriums.

✚ G6 ✉ 170 N. Dearborn Street ☎ 312/443–3800 🚇 Blue line: Washington 🚌 22, 24, 36, 62

ORCHESTRA HALL

From September to May the renowned Chicago Symphony Orchestra (CSO) is in residence in this sumptuous Greek Revival hall, built in 1904. Although tickets are snapped up early, some are available on the day of performance. The Civic Orchestra of Chicago, a training orchestra that often gives free concerts, and the Chicago Symphony Chorus also appear here.

✚ H7 ✉ 220 S. Michigan Avenue ☎ 312/294–3000 🚇 Brown, Orange lines: Adams 🚌 1, 3, 4, 6, 7, 38, 60

SECOND CITY

Biting satire and inspired improvisation have long been the stock-in-trade here, and they have been so successful that a second Second City theater now offers a different show simultaneously.

✚ G3 ✉ 1616 N. Wells Street ☎ 773/337–3992 🚇 Brown line: Sedgwick 🚌 11, 156

SHUBERT THEATER

Dating back to the 19th century, the handsome Shubert is a rare reminder that theater once thrived in the Loop. Dance companies perform here, though it is not exclusively a dance theater. It is best known for its musicals.

✚ G6 ✉ 22 W. Monroe Street ☎ 312/977–1701 🚇 Brown, Orange lines: Madison/Wells

STEPPENWOLF THEATER

Home of the enormously successful and influential Steppenwolf repertory company, founded in 1976, and still a premier venue for the best of Off-Loop theater. The theater has a 900-seat main hall and a smaller space for experimental drama.

✚ F3 ✉ 1650 N. Halsted Street ☎ 312/335–1650 🚇 Red line: North/Clybourn 🚌 8, 72

THEATER BUILDING

One of the city's most dependable venues for new drama, with three modest performance spaces often simultaneously occupied by local companies.

✚ Off map to north ✉ 1225 W. Belmont Avenue ☎ 773/327–5252 🚇 Brown, Red lines: Belmont 🚌 22

VICTORY GARDENS THEATER

Showcasing works of aspiring Chicago playwrights since 1974.

✚ F2 ✉ 2257 N. Lincoln Avenue ☎ 773/871–3000 🚇 Brown, Red lines: Fullerton 🚌 11

Half-price theater tickets

Hot Tix (✉ 108 N. State Street or Chicago Place, 700 N. Michigan Avenue) offers half-price tickets for many of the day's theater events. A recorded message (☎ 312/977–1755) lists the day's performances. Full-price advance tickets are also available from Hot Tix, as well as from another agency, Ticketmaster (☎ 312/559–1212 to charge by phone, ☎ 312/559–8989 for information).

Comedy shows

Two comedy shows have been entertaining Chicago theater-goers for years. Tony 'n' Tina's Wedding (✉ 230 W. North Avenue ☎ 312/664–8844), which started out in New York, re-creates an Italian-American wedding; the performers mingle with the audience ("the guests"). Meanwhile, Late Nite Catechism (✉ Royal George Theater, 1641 N. Halsted ☎ 312/988–9000) is a one-woman-show in which a nun recounts her American-Catholic upbringing, with audience participation.

NIGHTCLUBS

Nightclub news

The most general source is the Friday edition of the *Chicago Tribune*. Inside info on the latest clubs, as well as the nightlife scene in general, can be found in the pages of the weekly *Chicago Reader*, *New City*, and *UR*, all free of charge.

BERLIN

This big and immensely popular gay and lesbian nightspot puts on regular themed nights. It's packed to bursting on Fridays and Saturdays.

✚ Off map to north ✉ 954 W. Belmont Avenue ☎ 773/348–4975 🚇 Brown, Red lines: Belmont 🚌 77

BIOLOGY BAR

Three bars and a dance floor—9,000sq feet pulsate with Latin and salsa.

✚ F3 ✉ 1520 N. Fremont Street ☎ 312/266–1234 🚇 Red line: North/Clybourn 🚌 8

CROBAR

The city's leading nightspot for trance, house, and techno DJs; the place is packed on the weekend. Usually closed Monday and Tuesday.

✚ F5 ✉ 1543 N. Kingsbury Street ☎ 312/413–7000 🚇 Brown line: Chicago 🚌 37, 125

DRINK

A riotous restaurant and bar in the former meatpacking district that later becomes a dance venue with throbbing live music. Popular with people who work the nearby financial institutions.

✚ F6 ✉ 702 W. Fulton Street ☎ 312/733–7800 🚌 56

EXCALIBUR

This complex of billiards, pinball, video games, discos, and a restaurant is incongruously set in a 19th-century pseudo-Gothic castle, a sturdy granite structure built in the 1890s for the Chicago Historical Society. A favorite with twenty-somethings.

✚ G5 ✉ 632 N. Dearborn Street ☎ 312/266–1944 🚇 Red line: Grand 🚌 22

JILLY'S RETRO CLUB

Being dressed smartly and aged 25 or over are prerequisites for entry to Jilly's; being rich helps, too, as does a belief that the disco sounds of the 1970s were dance music's finest moments.

✚ H4 ✉ 1009 N. Rush Street ☎ 312/664–1001 🚇 Red line: Chicago 🚌 36

NEO

An ultra-cool crowd laps up sounds ranging from industrial dance and techno to slightly more mainstream music. By city nightlife standards, this is an old-timer.

✚ G2 ✉ 2350 N. Clark Street ☎ 773/528–2622 🚇 Brown, Red lines: Fullerton 🚌 22, 36

SPY BAR

Patrons dress in swanky club gear to edge past the bouncers, then sip Martinis before grooving to house music—the Spy Bar specialty. Sink into a velvet couch when you need a breather. Valet parking available.

✚ G2 ✉ 2350 N. Clark Street ☎ 773/528–2622 🚇 Brown, Red lines: Fullerton 🚌 22, 36

BARS

BILLY GOAT TAVERN

This below-street-level unpretentious watering hole is a favorite among local journalists.

✚ H5 ✉ 430 N. Michigan Avenue ☎ 312/222–1525 Ⓜ Red line: Grand 🚍 145, 146, 147, 151

COQ D'OR

Buddy Charles presides at this piano bar in the Drake Hotel.

✚ H4 ✉ 140 E. Walton Place ☎ 800/5–DRAKE or 312/787–2200 Ⓜ Red line: Chicago 🚍 145, 146, 147, 151

GAMEKEEPERS TAVERN & GRILL

A rowdy sports bar packed with televisions and raucous, twenty-something drinkers.

✚ G2 ✉ 1971 N. Lincoln Avenue ☎ 773/549–0400 Ⓜ Brown line: Armitage 🚍 11

HARRY CARAY'S

Created and named after the legendary baseball broadcaster who died in 1998, this sports bar is packed with baseball memorabilia. It's a great place to be after a Cubs win, and the Italian food is good.

✚ G5 ✉ 33 W. Kinzie Street ☎ 312/828–0966 Ⓜ Red line: Grand 🚍 62

JOHN BARLEYCORN MEMORIAL PUB

Established in the 1890s, this sizable pub not only slakes the thirst but provides classical music and a continuous slide show of works of art.

✚ F2 ✉ 658 W. Belden Avenue ☎ 773/348–8899 Ⓜ Brown, Red lines: Fullerton 🚍 11

POPS FOR CHAMPAGNE

A well-heeled and well-dressed crowd selects from a roster of champagnes in this stylish place. Light meals, live jazz.

✚ Off map to north ✉ 2934 N. Sheffield Avenue ☎ 773/472–1000 Ⓜ Brown line: Wellington 🚍 8

SHEFFIELD'S WINE & BEER

On a sunny day, make for the patio bar to sample the selection of microbrews, most made on the premises.

✚ Off map to north ✉ 3258 N. Sheffield Avenue ☎ 773/281–4989 Ⓜ Brown, Red lines: Belmont 🚍 9, 77

SHENANIGANS "H.O.B."

A promising selection of microbrewery beers from around the United States, in an ersatz fishing shack.

✚ G4 ✉ 16 W. Division Street ☎ 312/642–2344 Ⓜ Red line: Clark/Division 🚍 36, 70

WEEDS

Welcoming, anything-goes bar catering to artists, poets, misfits, and those who like drinking with them.

✚ F3 ✉ 1555 N. Dayton Street ☎ 312/943–7815 Ⓜ Red line: North/Clybourn 🚍 8

ZEBRA LOUNGE

An intimate piano bar with a loyal following. Open late most nights.

✚ G/H4 ✉ 1220 N. State Parkway ☎ 312/642–5140 Ⓜ Red line: Chicago 🚍 36

Liquor laws

Some bars serve liquor until 2AM every night except Saturday, when they may do so until 3AM on Sunday morning. Others continue serving until 4AM (5AM on Sunday mornings). The drinking age is 21, and stores may not sell liquor before noon on Sundays.

LUXURY HOTELS

Prices

Expect to pay the following prices per night for a double room:

Luxury—more than $200

Mid-Range—$120–$200

Budget—up to $120

Hostels—$15 per person

Many Chicago hotels offer weekend discounts, typically reducing the above prices by 20–40 percent.

CHICAGO HILTON & TOWERS

More than 1,600 rooms, a pervasive sense of grandeur, and the city's largest hotel health club.

✚ H7 ⊠ 720 S. Michigan Avenue ☎ 800/HILTONS or 312/922–4400; fax 312/922–5240 🚇 Red line: Harrison 🚌 1, 3, 4, 6, 146

THE DRAKE

Modeled on an Italian Renaissance palace, and opened in 1920, this is among Chicago's finest hotels. Some of the 537 rooms have lake views.

✚ H4 ⊠ 140 E. Walton Place ☎ 800/55–DRAKE or 312/787–2200; fax 312/397–1948 🚇 Red line: Chicago 🚌 145, 146, 147, 151

EMBASSY SUITES

385 suites in a good location for Michigan Avenue shopping and River North nightlife. Substantial buffet breakfast and a free evening cocktail party are included.

✚ G5 ⊠ 600 N. State Street ☎ 312/943–3800 or 800/EMBASSY; fax 312/943–7629 🚇 Red line: Grand 🚌 36

FAIRMONT HOTEL

Winning views over Grant Park, downtown, and the lake; the 672 rooms are comfortable and tasteful. Use of neighboring health club.

✚ H6 ⊠ 200 N. Columbus Drive ☎ 800/527–4727 or 312/565–8000; fax 312/565–1143 🚇 Brown, Orange lines: State, Lake 🚌 4

FOUR SEASONS

Excellent service and 343 traditional rooms. Rooftop running track.

✚ H4 ⊠ 120 E. Delaware Place ☎ 800/332–3442 or 312/280–8800; fax 312/280–1748 🚇 Red line: Chicago 🚌 145, 146, 147, 151

HYATT ON PRINTER'S ROW

Small and stylish; 161 rooms in two historic buildings.

✚ G7 ⊠ 500 S. Dearborn Street ☎ 800/233–1234 or 312/986–1234; fax 312/939–2468 🚇 Red line: Harrison 🚌 24, 36

RENAISSANCE CHICAGO

The convenient Loop location and the 553 spacious, well-equipped rooms make this a good choice for business travelers. Large lobby and bar.

✚ H6 ⊠ 1 W. Wacker Drive ☎ 800/468–3571 or 312/372–7200; fax 312/372–0093 🚇 Red line: Lake, State; Brown, Green lines: State 🚌 2, 10, 11, 44

RITZ-CARLTON

Traditional luxury above a chic mall. 435 rooms.

✚ H5 ⊠ 160 E. Pearson Street ☎ 800/621–6906 or 312/266–1000; fax 312/266–1194 🚇 Red line: Chicago 🚌 157

THE WHITEHALL

First opened in the 1920s, this 221-room hotel now has English-style furnishings, and two-line phone and fax machines.

✚ H4 ⊠ 105 E. Delaware Place ☎ 800/323–7500 or 312/944–6300; fax 312/944–8552 🚇 Red line: Chicago 🚌 145, 146, 147, 151

MID-RANGE HOTELS

THE ALLEGRO
The 483 rooms are easily the best-priced on the Loop.

✚ G6 ✉ 171 W. Randolph Street ☎ 800/643–1500 or 312/236–0123; fax 312/236–0917 🚇 Brown, Orange lines: Randolph/Wells 🚌 37

THE BURNHAM
Creative use of the historic Reliance Building (▶ 54) has yielded 122 comfortable if slightly cramped rooms. The Loop location is inspiring.

✚ H6 ✉ 1 W. Washington Street ☎ 312/782–1111 or 877/294–9712; fax 312/783–0899 🚇 Blue, Red lines: Washington 🚌 147, 151

CITY SUITES HOTEL
Most of the 45 accommodations are suites—and good value. A lively (if occasionally noisy) shopping and nightlife strip is on the doorstep.

✚ Off map to north ✉ 933 W. Belmont Avenue ☎ 773/404–3400 or 800/CITY–108; fax 773/404–3405 🚇 Brown, Red lines: Belmont 🚌 77

COURTYARD BY MARRIOTT
The 334 large, comfortable, well-priced rooms are designed for business travelers. The Loop is nearby.

✚ G5 ✉ 30 E. Hubbard Street ☎ 800/321–2211 or 312/329–2500; fax 312/329–0293 🚇 Red line: Grand 🚌 36

THE KNICKERBOCKER
Built in 1927, and now renovated, this 305-room hotel is close to the southern end of the Magnificent Mile. A secret stairwell on the 14th story is a legacy of the Prohibition era.

✚ H4 ✉ 163 E. Walton Street ☎ 800/621–8140 or 312/751–8100; fax 312/751–9205 🚇 Red line: Chicago 🚌 36

THE RAPHAEL
Tremendous value in an otherwise costly district, just off the Magnificent Mile. Most of the 172 rooms are suites including their own refrigerators.

✚ H4 ✉ 201 E. Delaware Place ☎ 800/983–7870 or 312/943–5000; fax 312/943–9483 🚇 Red line: Chicago 🚌 145, 146, 147, 151

TALBOTT HOTEL
The Talbott was built in 1927 as an apartment building, and most of the 149 rooms still have a kitchen. There is no restaurant, but the room-service menu is long.

✚ H4 ✉ 20 E. Delaware Place ☎ 800/825–2688 or 312/944–4970; fax 312/944–7241 🚇 Red line: Grand 🚌 36

TREMONT HOTEL
This elegant 130-room Tudor-style hotel is a stone's throw from Michigan Avenue shopping. Piano bar and fitness center.

✚ H4 ✉ 100 E. Chestnut Street ☎ 312/751–1900; fax 312/751–8691 🚇 Red line: Chicago 🚌 145, 146, 147, 151

Reservations

Rooms can be reserved by phone, fax, or mail; book as early as possible. A deposit (usually by credit card) equivalent to the nightly rate will ensure your room is held at least until 6PM; inform the hotel if you are arriving later. Credit card is the usual payment method; traveler's checks or cash can be used but payment might then be expected in advance. The total charge will include the city's 14.9 percent sales and room tax.

BUDGET ACCOMMODATIONS

Bed and breakfast

Bed-and-breakfasts offer an interesting alternative to hotels. They are typically Victorian homes fitted out in sumptuous style and filled with antiques. B&Bs span all price categories and are in many areas of Chicago, with a particularly strong concentration in Oak Park. The Bed & Breakfast Chicago agency (✉ PO Box 14088, Chicago, Illinois 60614 ☎ 800/375–7084 or 773/248–0085) operates a reservation system; it handles properties that are usually centrally located.

BEST WESTERN RIVER NORTH

The 145 rooms are good-value if unexciting. Rooftop pool. Close to the nightspots of River North. Restaurant.
✚ G5 ✉ 125 W. Ohio Street ☎ 800/727–0800 or 312/467–0800; fax 312/467–1665 Ⓡ Red line: Grand ⊟ 22

CASS HOTEL

Once past the forlorn lobby and the shabby downstairs bar you will find 158 clean rooms at a budget price within easy reach of the Magnificent Mile and River North.
✚ H5 ✉ 640 N. Wabash Avenue ☎ 800/787–4041 or 312/787–4030; fax 312/787–8544 Ⓡ Red line: Grand ⊟ 29, 65

THE CLARIDGE

Dating from the 1930s, this small hotel in the Gold Coast has good weekend rates and a good restaurant.
✚ G4 ✉ 1244 N. Dearborn Street ☎ 800/245–1258 or 312/787–4980; fax 312/266–0978 Ⓡ Red line: Clark/Division ⊟ 36

DAYS INN LINCOLN PARK NORTH

A 133-room motel at the busy intersection of Broadway, Clark, and Diversey, and a stone's throw from Wrigley Field. Free passes to the Bally's health club next door.
✚ F1 ✉ 644 W. Diversey Parkway ☎ 773/525–7010 or 800/DAYSINN; fax 773/525–6998 Ⓡ Brown line: Diversey ⊟ 22

HOSTEL CHICAGO INTERNATIONAL

Over 100 beds in dormitories and double rooms, several miles north of the center but with good public transportation links. To be closer to the city, use the Hostelling International property spread over seven floors on the south side of the Loop.
Hostel Chicago:
✚ Off map to north ✉ 6318 N. Winthrop Avenue ☎ 773/262–1011; fax 773/262–3673 Ⓡ Red line: Loyola ⊟ 155
Hostelling International:
✚ H7 ✉ 24 E. Congress Parkway ☎ 312/360–0300 Ⓡ Red line: Harrison ⊟ 6, 146

OHIO HOUSE

Dependable, simple motel with 50 rooms and exceptional rates in a River North location. Adjoining coffee shop.
✚ G5 ✉ 600 N. La Salle Street ☎ 312/943–6000; fax 312/943–6063 Ⓡ Red line: Grand ⊟ 37, 41

WILLOWS HOTEL

55 great-value rooms on a residential street in Lake View, close to the lake, Lincoln Park, and numerous bars and restaurants. The building dates from the 1920s and is full of character—the lobby is especially charming, with a fireplace and high windows.
✚ Off map to north ✉ 555 W. Surf Street ☎ 773/528–8400 or 800/SURF108 Ⓡ Brown line: Diversey ⊟ 36

CHICAGO
travel facts

PLANNING YOUR TRIP

When to go

- June, July, and August are the busiest months.
- May, September, and October are better months to visit, when there are fewer crowds and warm but less extreme weather.
- Events and festivals take place throughout the year (► 22). Most open-air events happen between spring and fall; many top cultural events occur in winter.
- Major conventions cause hotel space to be scarce; August, September, and October are peak convention months.

Climate

- Summers are hot and humid; winters are cold with snow; spring is mild but short; fall is mild and pleasant— September, October, and early November have the best weather.
- Be prepared for warm days and chilly evenings between April and October.
- Weather is changeable at any time; bring an umbrella and raincoat. Most rainfall is from April to September, but winters feel wetter.
- The wind is always there. It comes sweeping off the lake, and is particularly brutal in winter.

ARRIVING & DEPARTING

Arriving by air

- All American airlines, most international airlines, and some regional carriers serve Chicago.
- Chicago's O'Hare International Airport ☎ 773/686–2200 is 17 miles northwest of the Loop. One of the largest and busiest airports in the world, it handles all international flights and most domestic flights.
- Chicago Midway Airport ☎ 773/767–0600 is 8 miles southwest of the Loop. It is a quieter alternative for domestic flights, without the crowds and confusion of O'Hare.
- Meigs Field ☎ 312/744–4787, south of downtown, serves commuter airlines and operates flights to downstate Illinois and Wisconsin.
- Continental Air Transport ☎ 312/454–7799 runs minibuses between O'Hare and the Loop every five minutes from 6AM to 11:30PM; fare $17. From Midway, minibuses to the Loop leave every 15–20 minutes; fare $12.
- Chicago Transit Authority ☎ 888/YOUR-CTA runs Blue Line trains between O'Hare and the Loop around the clock. The journey takes around 35 minutes; the fare is about $1.50. From Midway, Orange line trains make the 30-minute ride to the Loop; fare about $1.50.
- Taxis wait at the arrivals terminal at O'Hare and Midway airports. The fare to the Loop or nearby hotels is $30–$35 from O'Hare and $20–$23 from Midway. A Shared-Ride option (from O'Hare or Midway airports) costs $15 or $10 respectively each.
- The flight time from New York to Chicago is about two hours and from Los Angeles about four hours.

Arriving by bus

- Greyhound buses into Chicago arrive at 630 W. Harrison Street, six blocks southwest of the Loop, and at neighborhood stations at the 95th Street and Dan Ryan Expressway CTA station, and at the Cumberland CTA station near O'Hare Airport. The Harrison Street terminal is quite a way from the main hotels area.
- Information ☎ 800/231–2222 or 312/781–2900

Arriving by train

- Amtrak trains use Chicago's Union Station, junction of W. Adams and S. Canal streets, two blocks west of the Loop.
- Information ☎ 800/872–7245 or 312/665–2385

Arriving by car

- Chicago has good interstate highway access: I-80 and I-90 are the major east–west routes; I-55 and I-57 arrive from the south. I-94 runs through the city linking the north and south suburbs.
- To reach the Loop from O'Hare airport use I-90/94. From Midway airport take I-55, linking with the northbound I-90/94 for the Loop. These rides should take about 45–90 minutes and 30–60 minutes respectively, all depending on traffic conditions.
- Try not to arrive during rush hours, 7–9AM and 4–7PM.

Departure and airport tax

- Departure and airport tax are included in the cost of your plane ticket.

ESSENTIAL FACTS

Etiquette

- Smoking is banned in all public buildings and transportation, and in movie theaters. It is also banned or restricted in many hotels and restaurants.
- Tipping is voluntary but the following tips are usually expected: 15 percent-plus in restaurants; 15–20 percent for taxis; $1–$2 per bag for a hotel porter, $1 for the doorman who gets you a cab.

Money matters

- Most banks have Automatic Teller Machines (ATMs).
- Credit cards are widely accepted.
- An 8.75 percent sales tax is added to marked retail prices, except on groceries and prescription drugs.

Places of Worship

- Baptist: Unity Fellowship Baptish Church ✉ 211 N. Cicero Avenue ☎ 773/287–0267; services Sun 8:15AM, 11:15AM, 5PM
- Jewish: Chicago Loop Synagogue ✉ 16 S. Clark Street ☎ 312/346–7370; services Mon–Fri 8:05AM
- Episcopal: Grace Episcopal Church ✉ 637 S. Dearborn Street ☎ 312/922–1426; services Wed 12:15PM; Sun 8AM, 11AM
- Methodist: Chicago Temple First United Methodist Church ✉ 77 W. Washington Boulevard ☎ 312/236–4548; services Sat 5pm; Sun 8:30, 11AM
- Catholic: Old St. Mary's Church ✉ 21 E Van Buren Street ☎ 312/922–3444; services Mon–Fri 7:15am, 12:10pm; Sat noon, 5PM; 8AM, 10:30AM, noon Sun.

Student travelers

- An International Student Identity Card (ISIC) reduces admission to many museums and other attractions.
- Anyone aged under 21 is forbidden to buy or drink liquor and may be denied admission to some nightclubs.
- For information on student services within the U.S. contact the Council on International Educational Exchange (CIEE) ✉ 205 E. 42nd Street, New York, NY 10017 ☎ 212/822–2600 or 888/268–6245

Time differences

- Chicago operates under U.S. Central Standard Time (CST) and is one hour behind the East Coast and two hours ahead of the West Coast.

Tourist information

- Visitor centers are inside Chicago Water Works ✉ 163 E. Pearson Street ☎ 312/744–2400; at the Chicago Cultural Center ✉ 77 E. Randolph Street ☎ 312/744– 2400, and at Illinois Market Place ✉ Navy Pier, 700 E. Grand Avenue. All are open daily but may close on holidays.
- Public library: Harold Washington Library Center ✉ 400 S. State Street ☎ 312/747–4300

PUBLIC TRANSPORTATION

- Much of Chicago can be explored on foot. To travel between neighborhoods use the network of buses and El (elevated railroad) trains, which travel above and below ground, and buses.
- El trains operate 24 hours a day.

- Metra commuter trains are best for visiting some areas.
- For information on the El and buses contact:
  Chicago Transit Authority ☎ 800/YOUR CTA
  Metra ☎ 312/322–6777 ⏱ Mon–Fri 8–5, otherwise 312/836 7000

The El

- Fare: $1.50. Transfer to a different line (or to a bus) within two hours: 30¢ (free within Loop). A second transfer within the same two hours is free.
- Plastic transit cards are the simplest way to pay fares. Tokens and cash are the alternatives.
- Rechargeable transit cards— available in any value from $1.50–$91—can also be used on buses, as can visitor passes valid for 1 day ($5), 2 days ($9), 3 days ($12) or 4 days ($18).
- Stations have fare booths or automatic ticket machines.
- Six color-coded lines (▶ 6) run through the city in different directions, all of them converging on the Loop.
- On weekdays between 6AM and 7PM, trains on most lines stop only at alternate stations, plus all major stations. Check whether you need the A service or the B service.
- Most trains run 24 hours, less frequently on weekends and late in the evenings.
- Some stations close on weekends.

Buses

- Fare: $1.50. Transfer to a different route (or to the El) within two hours: 30¢.

A second transfer made within the same two hours is free.

- Plastic transit cards are the simplest way to pay fares. Tokens and cash (exact change only) are the alternatives.
- Rechargeable transit cards—available in any value from $1.50–$91—can also be used on the El as can visitor passes valid for 1 day ($5), 2 days ($9), 3 days ($12) or 4 days ($18).

Schedule and map information

- CTA maps showing both El routes and bus routes are available from El station fare booths.
- Bus routes are shown at all stops.

Taxis

- Hail them on the street or get one outside hotels, conference centers, and major El stations.
- Fares are $1.60 plus $1.40 per mile and 50¢ each for more than one passenger. An additional charge may be made for waiting time.
- Hotel, restaurant, and nightclub staff will order a taxi on request; or you can phone American United ☎ 312/248–7600; Checker ☎ 312/243–2537; Yellow ☎ 312/829–4222

Driving

- Rush hours are 7–9AM and 4–7.
- Many hotels have parking lots for guests; otherwise overnight parking is difficult and very costly. During the day, street parking is often limited to two hours; spaces in the Loop are virtually impossible to find.
- Driving in the city is stressful: the best option is to use public transportation.
- For highway driving conditions call the Illinois Department of Transportation ☎ 312/793–2242 or 800/452–IDOT

Car rental

- Car-rental companies based at airports may be more expensive than others. The best option is to use the free shuttle service to rental lots outside the airport.
- Main car-rental agencies: Alamo ☎ 800/327–8017 Avis ☎ 800/327–9633 Budget ☎ 800/527–0700 Dollar ☎ 800/800–4000 Hertz ☎ 800/604–3131 National InterRent ☎ 800/227–7368

Media & Communications

Magazines

- Magazines include *Chicago*, a glossy monthly that speaks to the well-heeled Chicagoan; *Windy City Times*, which is pitched at gays and lesbians; and free magazines such as *Chicago Key*, found in hotel lobbies and designed for tourists.
- A wide range of overseas newspapers and magazines can be found at Barnes & Noble and Borders Books & Music stores (► 75).

Newspapers

- Major daily newspapers are: the *Chicago Tribune*, which

91

covers international, national, and local issues; and the tabloid *Chicago Sun-Times*, which concentrates on local stories.

- The best of several free weeklies is the *Chicago Reader*, which has a mix of local news, features, and entertainment listings.

Post offices

- Main post office ✉ 433 W. Harrison Street
  To find the nearest post office, look in the phone book or ask at your hotel. Most are open Mon–Fri 8:30–5, Sat 8:30–1. For information ☎ 312/765–32310

Radio

- Alternative rock: Q101 101FM, WXRT 93FM
- Classical: WFMT 98.7FM
- Country: WUSN 99.5FM
- Jazz: WNUA 95.5FM
- National Public Radio: WBEZ 91.5FM
- News: WBBM 780AM, WMAQ 670AM
- Rock: WCKG 105.9FM
- R&B: WGCI 107.5FM
- Talk radio and local sports: WGN 820AM

Telephones

- Public telephones are found on the street and in hotel lobbies, restaurants, and public buildings. Local calls cost 35¢.
- Calls from hotel rooms are usually more expensive than calls made from public telephones.
- Area codes: 312 (downtown); 773 (rest of the city); 708 (southwest suburbs); 630 (western suburbs); 847 (north and northwest suburbs). Codes have already been applied to the numbers throughout this book.
- Long-distance services:
  AT&T ☎ 800/222–0300
  MCI ☎ 800/955–5555
  Sprint ☎ 800/877–7746

Television

- The main Chicago TV channels are 2 WBBM (CBS), 5 WMAQ (NBC), 7 WLS (ABC), 9 WGN (local WB affiliate), 11 WTTW (PBS).
- Most hotels provide cable TV and pay-per-view movies.

EMERGENCIES

Emergency telephone numbers

- Fire, police or ambulance:
  ☎ 911 (no money required)
- Rape Crisis Hotline
  ☎ 888/293–2080

Lost property

- O'Hare International Airport
  ☎ 312/686–2200
- Lost in a cab ☎ 312/744–2900 or 312/744–6227
- The El and buses:
  Chicago Transit Authority
  ☎ 1-888/YOUR CTA
  Metra ☎ 312/322–6777 (Mon–Fri 8–5) otherwise 312/836–7000

Medical treatment

- If you need a doctor, ask at your hotel or contact the non-emergency Medical Referral Service ☎ 312/670–2550
- Hospitals with 24-hour emergency rooms include: Northwestern Memorial Hospital ✉ 233 E. Superior Street ☎ 312/908–2000
- The Chicago Dental Association ☎ 312/836–7300 makes referrals.

Medicines

- Pharmacies are listed in *Yellow Pages*.
- Late-night pharmacies in the city include Walgreen's ✉ 757 N. Michigan Avenue ☎ 800/925–4733 🕐 24 hours. Osco Drug has a toll-free number ☎ 888/443–5701 giving the location of its nearest 24-hour branch.

Consulates

- Canadian ✉ Suite 2400, 180 N. Stetson Avenue ☎ 312/616–1860
- Germany ✉ Suite 3200, 676 N. Michigan Avenue ☎ 312/580–1199
- Ireland ✉ Suite 911, Wrigley Building, 400 N. Michigan Avenue ☎ 312/337–1868
- U.K. ✉ Suite 1300, Wrigley Building, 400 N. Michigan Avenue ☎ 312/346–1810

Sensible precautions

- Observe commonsense precautions.
- By day, the Loop and major areas of interest to visitors are relatively safe. Some tourist sites involve traveling through unwelcoming areas; be wary on the South Side and Near West Side or on the El at night.
- Discuss your itinerary with hotel staff and heed their advice.
- After dark, stick to established nightlife areas. River North and River West, Rush and Division streets, and Wrigleyville/Lake View, are relatively safe. Public transportation is generally safe between these areas.
- Stick to busy streets. Neighborhoods can change character within a few blocks.
- Solo travelers, including women, are not unusual in Chicago. Women may encounter unwanted attention; if waiting for a cab, do so inside the club or restaurant, or where staff can see you.
- Carry shoulder bags strapped across your chest, and keep your wallet in your front trouser pocket or chest pocket. In a bar, restaurant, or movie theater, keep belongings within sight and within reach. Women should never let their handbag dangle from the back of their chair in a restaurant.
- Store valuables in your hotel safe and never carry more money than you need for the day. Most purchases can be made with traveler's checks or credit cards.
- Lost traveler's checks are relatively easy to replace.
- Report any item that has been stolen to the nearest police precinct (addresses are in the phone book). It is unlikely that any stolen goods will be recovered but the police will be able to fill out the forms that your insurance company needs.

INDEX

Citypack
Chicago

AUTHOR *Mick Sinclair*
COVER DESIGN *Tigist Getachew*
COVER PICTURES *AA Photo Library*
MANAGING EDITOR *Jackie Staddon*

Copyright   © Automobile Association Developments Limited 1997, 1999, 2001
Maps   © Automobile Association Developments Limited 1997, 1999, 2001
Fold-out map: © RV Reise- und Verkehrsverlag Munich · Stuttgart
    © Cartography: GeoData

ISBN 0-676–90154–9
Revised Third Edition

Acknowledgments

The Automobile Association wishes to thank the following libraries and institutes for their assistance in the preparation of this book: The Art Institute of Chicago 40b; The Bridgeman Art Library, London 36, scene from 'The Last of the Mohicans' (New York Historical Society); Chicago Board of Trade 31a; Mary Evans Picture Library 12; The Glessner House Museum, courtesy of Prairie Avenue House Museums, Chicago 43; Frank Lloyd Wright Home & Studio Foundation 24a, 24b; The University of Chicago 47a, 47b. The remaining photographs are held in the Association's own library (AA Photo Library) and were taken by Phil Wood with the exception of page 56 taken by Sean M. Taylor.

Important tip

Time inevitably brings changes, so always confirm prices, travel facts, and other perishable information when it matters. Although Fodor's cannot accept responsibility for errors, you can use this guide in the confidence that we have taken every care to ensure its accuracy.

Special sales

Fodor's Travel Publications are available at special discounts for bulk purchases (100 copies or more) for sales promotions or premiums. Special editions, including personalized covers, excerpts of existing guides, and corporate imprints, can be created in large quantities for special needs. For more information contact your local bookseller or write to Special Marketing, Fodor's Travel Publications, 280 Park Avenue, New York, NY 10017. Inquiries from Canada should be directed to your local Canadian bookseller or sent to Random House of Canada, Ltd., Marketing Department, 2775 Matheson Blvd. East, Mississauga, Ontario L4W 4P7.

Color separation by Daylight Colour Art Pte Ltd, Singapore
Manufactured by Dai Nippon Printing Co. (Hong Kong) Ltd

10 9 8 7 6 5 4 3 2 1

Titles in the Citypack series